Generis
PUBLISHING

Pedagogy of Kindness

Changing Lives, Changing the World

Elizabeth Gorny-Wegrzyn (First Author)
Beth Perry

Title: Pedagogy of Kindness

Changing Lives, Changing the World

ISBN: 978-1-63902-936-5

Author: Elizabeth Gorny-Wegrzyn (First Author), Beth Perry

Cover image: www.pixabay.com

Publisher: Generis Publishing
Online orders: www.generis-publishing.com
Contact email: info@generis-publishing.com

Dedication

This book is dedicated to Dr. Colleen M. Stanton, and educators like her, who embrace a pedagogy of kindness in all their actions and interactions with learners. Dr. Stanton, who contributed a chapter featured in this book, died suddenly just after completing a draft of her manuscript. We are thankful for gifted educators like Colleen who live by the fundamental principles of a pedagogy of kindness, "Believing people, and believing in people" (Denial, 2019).

Figure 1.

Pedagogy of kindness word picture

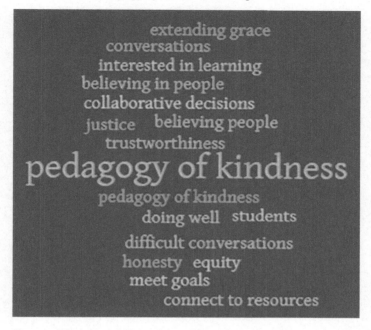

Note – From (Vickey, 2021) https://uwm.edu/graduateschool/that-kind-of-teacher-alum-returns-to-uwm-to-spread-a-pedagogy-of-kindness/

Reference

Vickey, S. (2021). *What kind of teacher: Alum returns to UWM to spread a pedagogy of kindness.* https://uwm.edu/graduateschool/that-kind-of-teacher-alum-returns-to-uwm-to-spread-a-pedagogy-of-kindness/

Authors

Elizabeth Gorny-Wegrzyn RN, MN is a recent graduate of the Master of Nursing program from Athabasca University and works as a nurse in oncology in Quebec, Canada.

Beth Perry RN, PhD is a Professor in the Faculty of Health Disciplines at Athabasca University in Alberta, Canada.

Collen Stanton PhD was an instructor in the Faculty of Health Disciplines graduate programs at Athabasca University.

Katherine Janzen MN is a graduate of the Faculty of Health Disciplines Master of Nursing program and a recent faculty member at Mount Royal University School of Nursing and Midwifery.

Regan Hack RN, MN is an educator in the Faculty of Health Disciplines at Athabasca University.

Table of Contents

Chapter Seven: *How the Pedagogy of Kindness Can Accentuate the Advantages and Minimize the Limitations of Online Education*

Preface:

The Use of Kindness in Pedagogy

By Elizabeth Gorny-Wegrzyn

Overview of a Pedagogy of Kindness

"Sometimes it takes only one act of kindness and caring to change a person's life." (Chan, 2017).

Through recent decades, educators, theorists, and academics have researched the science of learning and tried to find teaching approaches that engage and motivate students and improve learning outcomes, both in traditional classrooms and in an online milieu. In these studies, a prevalent theme emerged that demonstrates that embracing kindness as a teaching philosophy communicates to students that they have meaning and are valued. For example, when students feel worthwhile and valued, they try harder and do better at their studies, and feel more worthy as human beings (Serbati et al., 2020; Thomas, 2019).

That is not to say that there will never be disappointments with any given teaching approach. In supporting a nurturing learning environment of open communication, educators should expect some challenges given the various learning stressors and student individualities. These setbacks can become learning opportunities as educators find ways to welcome and appreciate learners with different backgrounds, beliefs, values, opinions, and cognitive levels. Using kindness, care, and compassion in pedagogy gives all students a chance to learn and to thrive as individuals.

What is a pedagogy of kindness (PofK)? A PofK is a teaching philosophy based on teachers being accessible, welcoming, collaborative, and respectful (Rawle, 2021). Using kindness (and care, compassion, and empathy) as the foundation of a teaching philosophy encourages instructors and students to form sound educator-learner relationships based on trust and to collaborate as equals in the teaching-learning process (Denial, 2019; Serbati et al., 2020; Thomas, 2019). The PofK supports a learning environment that is empathetic to individual learner needs and promotes a sense of community, collaboration, and class partnership. A PofK enables students to improve the outcomes of their academic endeavors. This teaching philosophy also supports student-centered learning, respects differences in students' backgrounds and educational goals, and helps students feel valuable and worthwhile as human beings. (Denial, 2019; Serbati et al., 2020). Further, this pedagogy allows educators to appreciate students' contributions to the educational process as respected partners, thus affording teachers career fulfillment and satisfaction (Perry & Edwards, 2012; Serbati et al., 2020).

In the following chapters, we explore the benefits of using kindness, care, compassion, and empathy as pillars in a teaching philosophy. We examine in detail a pedagogy that is learner-centered, open, collaborative, respectful, and inviting to students. Specifically, we focused on the advantages of using the PofK in higher education. Additionally, other pedagogies created from the same foundations as the PofK are thoroughly discussed in subsequent chapters. We hope you enjoy this perspective on how teachers and students can work together as equal partners to be more successful and feel more satisfied in the teaching-learning process.

References

Chan, J. (2017). 30 inspiring kindness quotes that will enlighten you. https://www.ftd.com/blog/celebrate/kindness-quotes

Denial, C. (2019). *A pedagogy of kindness*. https://hybridpedagogy.org/pedagogy-of-kindness

Perry, B., & Edwards, M. (2012). Creating an "invitational classroom" in the online educational milieu. *American Journal of Health Sciences (AJHS)*, *3*(1), 7-16. https://doi.org/10.19030/ajhs.v3i1.6747

Rawle, F. (2021). Dr. Fiona Rawle on the pedagogy of kindness. *The Medium*. https://themedium.ca/features/the-pedagogy-of-kindness/

Serbati, A., Aquario, D., Da Re, L., Paccagnella, O., & Felisatti, E. (2020). Exploring good teaching practices and needs for improvement: Implications for staff development. *Journal of Educational, Cultural and Psychological Studies (ECPS Journal)*, *21*, 43-64. https://doi.org/10.7358/ecps-2020-021-serb

Thomas, H. (2020). What are learning theories and why are they important for learning design? *My Brain is Open*.

https://www.mybrainisopen.net/learning-theories-and-learning-design/

Chapter One:

Theoretical Underpinnings: Links between the Pedagogy of Kindness and Learning Theories

By Elizabeth Gorny-Wegrzyn

Chapter one explores the connection of the PofK to other major learnings theories. First, we give a brief overview of three noteworthy theories, behaviourism, cognitivism, and constructivism. Second, we describe the links of the PofK to the constructivist learning theory. Finally, we connect the PofK to the learning theories that developed from the underpinnings of constructivism. The PofK and similar teaching theories all focus on the pillars of kindness, care, compassion, and empathy. The values foundational to these philosophies are learner-centred, collaborative, and inviting, and they include both teachers and students in decision-making as equal partners. Respecting and valuing the opinions and individualities of students is beneficial in creating an engaging and inviting class environment that facilitates more successful learning outcomes.

Chapter Objectives

After completing chapter one the reader will be able to

- Describe the three significant learning theories developed in the 20th century
- Explain the links of the PofK and constructivism
- Connect the PofK to similar teaching philosophies

Introduction/Background of Learning Theories

The 20th century gave rise to three significant learning theories, behaviourism, cognitivism, and constructivism (Harasim, 2017; Thomas, 2020). Behaviourism, created by Ivan Pavlov, was influenced by positivism, the scientific method, and psychology. Behaviourists propose that learning is "empirical, observable and measurable" (Harasim, 2017, Abstract, Ch. 3). Later, the cognitivist learning theory developed as an extension and adaptation of behaviourism. Cognitivism is less rigid and considers the social aspect of human behavior (Harasim, 2017). Finally, Jean Piaget was instrumental in developing the constructivist learning theory in the 1970s, during the educational and social reform period in the United States and Europe (Harasim, 2017). Constructivism is both a learning theory and an epistemology. This learning theory also takes into consideration how knowledge is constructed and understood. Constructivists propose that learners build knowledge rather than just passively taking in information. Individuals reflect upon their experiences, acquire new information when learning, and incorporate it into their pre-existing knowledge base (Harasim, 2017; University at Buffalo, 2021). All these learning theories have value and have positively influenced the educational process. Over the years, many teaching philosophies and pedagogies grew from these original learning theories.

Presently, educators have numerous pedagogies they can choose to incorporate into their practice depending on their teaching philosophy. The PofK is one such teaching philosophy shaped from emerging theories that have proven effective in engaging and motivating students and improving their academic outcomes, both in traditional classrooms and online.

The PofK and Constructivism

There are many similarities between the constructivist learning theory and the PofK. The theoretical underpinnings of the PofK came from the philosophy foundational to constructivism. Constructivist teaching philosophy is democratic and encourages students to be autonomous and to share authority with teachers (McLeod, 2019; Western Governors University, 2020). In the same sense, the PofK discourages hierarchal power structures in academia and promotes equal balances of power between students and teachers (Magnet et al., 2014). A constructivist classroom environment is student-centered and collaborative (McLeod, 2019; Western Governors University, 2020). Correspondingly, educators using a PofK believe that learning is inherently a social phenomenon and is done best with the collaboration of others (Clegg & Rowland, 2010). Constructivist class activities are interactive, and constructivist educators facilitate students to become "active participants in their own learning" (McLeod, 2019, para. What is the role). Similarly, teachers embracing the PofK encourage students to engage in classroom activities and invite them to discuss divergent thoughts, opinions, and values (Loreman, 2011).

Constructivist teachers act as facilitators of the educational process, encourage students to ask questions, and empower them to share authority in class decisions and control their thinking and learning (Gray, n. d.). Educators are empathetic towards students and try to understand their different viewpoints and preconceptions, thus advancing the learning process (McLeod, 2019). Clegg and Rowland (2010) write that educators who embrace a PofK must understand things from students' perspectives to help them meet their personal and academic needs. Loreman (2011) notes that teachers are partners with students in the learning process and help and support learners with genuine feeling. The instructors' feelings of empathy encompass all students, their diversity, and their individualities (Loreman, 2011). Finally, Magnet et al. (2014) write that kindness in pedagogy allows educators to engage with students, understand their differences and individual needs, and "build relationships of solidarity with students and each other" (p. 11). It is clear, therefore, that the foundations of the PofK are related to a constructivist philosophy. Both doctrines state that learners are valuable contributors and partners in the teaching and learning process, and both encourage critical thinking, collaboration with others, and learner autonomy.

The PofK and Invitational Learning Theory

The PofK can also be linked closely to Invitational Learning Theory (Purkey & Novak, 2015). Both teaching philosophies are student-centered, collaborative, and respect the individualities of learners. Invitational Learning Theory evolved from three foundations, the democratic ethos, the perceptual tradition, and the self-concept theory (Purkey & Novak, 2015). These three foundations could also be the underpinnings of the PofK.

Democratic ethos demonstrates implied respect for individuals who can make responsible decisions on events that impact their lives. Invitational Learning Theory uses reflective dialogue, mutual respect, and the importance of collaboration to illustrate this ethos (Purkey & Novak, 2015). Perceptual tradition proposes that human behaviour is dependent on individual perceptions of happenings in the world. To understand these behaviors, we must first understand these perceptions (Purkey & Novak, 2015). Finally, self-concept is a multifaceted belief system that individuals learn and believe to be true about themselves. These beliefs influence their behavior (Purkey & Novak, 2015). In the same sense, the PofK uses mutual respect, open discussion, and collaboration as foundations of its teaching philosophy. A PofK encourages educators to understand students' thoughts, perceptions, values, and opinions, an understanding that makes students feel valued. When students feel valued, their perceptions of themselves and the world are positive.

Invitational Learning Theory focuses on five elements in teaching: care, trust, respect, optimism, and intentionality (Purkey & Novak, 2015). These elements are crucial to creating and maintaining a learning environment that is effective and inviting. Care is the principal element and at the heart of this theory's perspective on teaching and learning (Purkey & Novak, 2015). Invitational Theory, built upon the five pillars of people, places, policies, programs, and processes, makes contributions that address the psychogeography and the constructive alignment of learning environments and the training of teachers and counselors (Purkey & Novak, 2015). Correspondingly, the PofK uses care, kindness, empathy, and compassion as the building blocks in its philosophy on teaching and is elemental in constructing learning environments that are warm, caring, and inviting towards its students and educators.

The PofK and Open Pedagogy (OP)

As with many collaborative learning philosophies that emerged from constructivism, the PofK affirms that students are collaborators in the teaching/learning process. Educators embracing this philosophy believe that learners make constructive and valuable contributions to the educational process and often design and modify class syllabi, assignments, and assessments according to student inputs (Henard & Roseveare, 2012). Teachers who adopt open pedagogy also nurture the construction of mutually trusting educator-learner relationships that create rich and satisfying learning environments and positively impact learning outcomes (Serbati et al., 2020). Likewise, PofK inspired learning environments consider and respect students' backgrounds, cultures, and unique life experiences and invite open discussions on various beliefs, opinions, perceptions, and values. These discussions encourage meaningful exchanges of ideas that offer insights into social injustices, increase social awareness, and lead to the achievement of social-emotional and affective domain learning outcomes (Magnet et al., 2014; Perry & Edwards, 2019).

The PofK, therefore, can also be aligned with Open Pedagogy (OP) as both teaching viewpoints promote collaborating with students as equal partners in the learning process. OP is a non-hierarchal approach to building competencies and promotes reciprocal learning between learners and teachers. OP empowers both educators and students to be co-producers and co-creators of knowledge. Specifically, The University of Texas (2016) defines OP as "the practice of engaging with students as creators of information rather than simply consumers of it. It is a form of experiential learning in which students demonstrate understanding through the act of creation" (para. 1).

OP also supports students to co-create open educational resources (OER) (University of Texas, 2016). OP empowers educators and learners to modify open-license textbooks and other learning material and share this co-created knowledge with others (BC Campus, n. d.; University of Saskatchewan, n. d.; University of Texas, 2016). In this sense, both the PofK and OP promote encouraging, inviting, and open class environments that nurture students, cultivate intellectual curiosity, and foster collaboration and a sense of classroom partnership.

The PofK and Positivity, Mindfulness, and Gratitude

An article in *Education's Voice* (2016) reports that one of the foundational elements in mindfulness is feeling grateful and appreciative of acts of kindness towards us and being willing to reciprocate. Being thankful for acts of support makes us mindful, or more aware, of the good factors in life. Gratitude, therefore, increases our awareness of the good in life and increases our feelings of well-being and positivity (*Education's Voice*, 2016).

Mindfulness, therefore, can be used in pedagogy to increase feelings of well-being in both students and educators. Wamsler et al. (2018) note that academics have begun to investigate theoretical models of mindful teaching and incorporate them into pedagogical practice. The authors define mindful teaching as "the building of a community or connection (teacher–student and student–student) based on compassion, non-judgmental, and accepting openness, and the establishment of respectful boundaries; and the creation of an engaging and reflective learning environment, which supports self-observation and mutual learning, whilst acknowledging differences in cultural backgrounds, experiences, social behavior, and learning" (Wamsler et al., 2018, para. Mindfulness in general sustainability teaching).

In the same sense, mindfulness in pedagogy is like the PofK teaching philosophy. The PofK is one of the teaching models that incorporates mindfulness into teaching practice. The PofK uses care, kindness, empathy, and compassion in its teaching method. Educators using the PofK encourage learning environments that are open, inviting and encouraging of collaborative study, and they are respectful of the unique backgrounds, thoughts, and experiences of students (Magnet et al., 2014; Perry & Edwards, 2019). Using a PofK or mindfulness as a teaching approach inspires students to be more self-reflective, compassionate, and just human beings (Wamsler et al., 2018).

The PofK and Effective Online Education

Due to the recent worldwide COVID-19 pandemic, an effective pedagogy must successfully transition from an in-class teaching method to an online approach as most academic institutions have gone exclusively online. This new focus on online teaching and learning as a credible alternative to in-person learning is likely to endure post-pandemic. Educators today need to be equally skilled at teaching in all learning environments including online. A PofK has attributes that support a teaching approach that is effective in an online milieu. Effective online instruction uses a constructivist philosophy where learning is an active process (Rieger et al., 2020). Skilled online educators adopt a wholly student-centered and collaborative teaching approach and address the unique needs of students learning at a distance (Bates, 2020; Rapanta et al., 2020). As noted earlier, a PofK is a philosophy that emerged from a constructivist point of view and is collaborative and respectful of students' unique individualities, making it likely to be successful online.

Example/scenario of PofK success: Arts-Based Instruction

In a case example, a student wrote about how the kindness and care of outstanding educators instilled in her feelings of worthiness instead of inadequacy and encouraged her to continue her studies and graduate (Gorny-Wegrzyn & Perry, 2021). The student reported that even small acts of kindness can make significant impacts on students' feelings, lives, and the academic successes of both learners and teachers (Gorny-Wegrzyn & Perry, 2021). An educator adopting a PofK as a teaching approach can build the groundwork for success by inspiring students to feel valued and worthy and by making classrooms environments welcoming, nurturing, and collaborative (Gorny-Wegrzyn & Perry, 2021; Perry & Edwards, 2012; Purkey & Novak, 2015; Serbati et al., 2020).

Innovative and engaging teaching strategies (i.e., visual aids, creative instructional strategies, and humour) sustain classroom activities and discussions, strengthen relationships, and help increase the achievement of social-emotional and affective domain learning outcomes (Perry & Edwards, 2012, 2019; Serbati et al., 2020). Educators espousing a PofK often use arts-based instruction (ABI), which is welcoming and collaborative and encourages students to voice their opinions and to listen to the views of others (Perry & Edwards, 2019). Arts-based teaching strategies such as photovoice, parallel poetry, and conceptual quilting can sustain interactions among students and between educators and learners, making these interactions "richer, more insightful, and more intimate" (Perry & Edwards, 2012, p. 12). ABI helps students share their opinions, views, life experiences, and values. Mutual sharing makes classroom environments inviting and collaborative and enhances trust in relationships (Perry & Edwards, 2012). These environments make students feel comfortable expressing their thoughts and make them feel appreciated (Perry & Edwards, 2012). ABI helps create a learning environment compatible with a PofK.

Conclusion/Summary

A PofK is effective as an educational philosophy, both for in-class and online instruction. The use of kindness, care, empathy, and compassion when teaching fosters learning environments that are inviting and collaborative and instills confidence and feelings of worth in students (Denial, 2019; Serbati et al., 2020; Thomas, 2019). This confidence and feeling of value motivate students to do better at their studies and facilitates academic success in both learners and educators (Serbati et al., 2020). A PofK does more than enhance educational success: it inspires learners to appreciate and value themselves and others. A PofK "helps build resilience and confidence in students making them better citizens and more compassionate human beings" (Gorny-Wegrzyn & Perry, 2021, para. Conclusion). Embracing a PofK as a teaching philosophy encourages students and educators to thrive academically and as human beings.

References

Bates, A. W. (2020). Advice to those about to teach online because of the corona-virus. *Online Learning and Distant Education Resources.* https://www.tonybates.ca/2020/03/09/advice-to-those-about-to-teach-online-because-of-the-corona-virus/.

BC Campus. (n.d.). What is open pedagogy? *OpenEd.* https://open.bccampus.ca/what-is-open-education/what-is-open-pedagogy/

Clegg, S., & Rowland, S. (2010). Kindness in pedagogical practice and academic life. *British Journal of Sociology of Education, 31*(6), 719-735. http://www.jstor.org/stable/25758494

Denial, C. (2019). *A pedagogy of kindness.* https://hybridpedagogy.org/pedagogy-of-kindness

Education's Voice. (2016). Mindfulness in the classroom: Gratitude. https://educationsvoice.wordpress.com/2016/02/18/mindfulness-in-the-classroom-gratitude/

FTD Fresh, (October 23, 2017). 30 inspiring kindness quotes that will enlighten you. *FTD by Design.* https://www.ftd.com/blog/celebrate/kindness-quotes

Gray, A. (n. d). Constructivist teaching and learning. *University of Saskatchewan.* https://saskschoolboards.ca/wp-content/uploads/97-07.htm#EXECUTIVE%20SUMMARY

Gorny-Wegrzyn, E. & Perry, B. (2021). Inspiring educators and a pedagogy of kindness: A reflective essay. *Creative Education, 12*(1). https://www.scirp.org/journal/paperinformation.aspx?paperid=106777

Groves, M., Sellars, C., Smith, J., & Barber, A. (2015). Factors affecting student engagement: A case study examining two cohorts of students attending a post-1992 university in the United Kingdom. *International Journal of Higher Education, 4*, 27-37. https://doi.org/10.5430/ijhe.v4n2p27

Harasim, L. (2017). *Learning theory and online technologies* (2nd edition). Routledge Ltd. https://doi.org/10.4324/9781315716831

Hativa, N., Barak, R., & Simhi, E. (2001). Exemplary university teachers: Knowledge and beliefs regarding effective teaching dimensions and strategies. *The Journal of Higher Education, 72,* 699-729. https://doi.org/10.1080/00221546.2001.11777122

Henard, F., & Roseveare, D. (2012). *Fostering quality teaching in higher education: Policies and practices.* Paris: OECD. https://www.oecd.org/education/imhe/QT%20policies%20and%20practices.pdf

Loreman, T. (2011). Kindness and Empathy in Pedagogy. In T. Loreman (Ed.), *Love as Pedagogy* (pp. 15-31). Rotterdam: Sense Publishers. https://doi.org/10.1007/978-94-6091-484-3

Magnet, S., Mason, C., & Trevenen, K. (2014). Feminism, pedagogy, and the politics of kindness. *Feminist Teacher, 25,* 1-22. https://doi.org/10.5406/femteacher.25.1.0001

McLeod, S. (2019). Constructivism as a theory for teaching and learning. *Simply Psychology.* https://www.simplypsychology.org/constructivism.html

Perry, B., & Edwards, M. (2012). Creating an "invitational classroom" in the online educational milieu. *American Journal of Health Sciences (AJHS), 3*(1), 7-16. https://doi.org/10.19030/ajhs.v3i1.6747

Perry, B., & Edwards, M. (2019). Innovative arts-based learning approaches adapted for mobile learning. *Open Praxis, 11*(3). https://doi.org/10.5944/openpraxis.11.3.967

Purkey, W. W., & Novak, J. M. (2015). An introduction to invitational theory. *invitationaleducation.org* https://www.invitationaleducation.org/wp-content/uploads/2019/04/art_intro_to_invitational_theory-1.pdf

Rapanta, C., Botturi, L., Goodyear, P. et al. (2020). Online university teaching during and after the Covid-19 crisis: Refocusing teacher presence and learning activity. *Postdigit Sci Educ, 2,* 923–945. https://doi.org/10.1007/s42438-020-00155-y

Rawle, F. (2021). Dr. Fiona Rawle on the pedagogy of kindness. *The Medium.* https://themedium.ca/features/the-pedagogy-of-kindness/

Rieger, K. L., Chernomas, W. M., McMillan, D. E., & Morin, F. L. (2020). Navigating creativity within arts-based pedagogy: Implications of a constructivist grounded theory study. *Nurse Education Today, 91.* https://doi.org/10.1016/j.nedt.2020.104465

Serbati, A., Aquario, D., Da Re, L., Paccagnella, O., & Felisatti, E. (2020). Exploring good teaching practices and needs for improvement: Implications for staff development. *Journal of Educational, Cultural and Psychological Studies (ECPS Journal), 21*, 43-64. https://doi.org/10.7358/ecps-2020-021-serb

Thomas, H. (2020). What are learning theories and why are they important for learning design? *My Brain is Open.* https://www.mybrainisopen.net/learning-theories-and-learning-design/

Thomas, W. (2019). *Pedagogy of Care.* https://willt486.github.io/teaching/2019/08/23/pedagogy-of-care

University at Buffalo. (2021). Constructivism. *Center for Educational Innovation.* http://www.buffalo.edu/ubcei/enhance/learning/constructivism.html

University of Saskatchewan. (n.d.). Open Pedagogy. *Teaching and Learning.* https://teaching.usask.ca/curriculum/open-pedagogy.php#OpenPedagogyandOurLearningCharter

University of Texas. (2016). Introduction to open pedagogy. *UTA Libraries.* https://libguides.uta.edu/openped

Wamsler, C., Brossmann, J., Hendersson, H. et al. (2018). Mindfulness in sustainability science, practice, and teaching. *Sustain Sci, 13*, 143–162. https://doi.org/10.1007/s11625-017-0428-2

Western Governors University. (2020, May 27). *What is constructivism?* https://www.wgu.edu/blog/what-constructivism2005.html#close

Chapter Two:

Inspiring Educators and a Pedagogy of Kindness:
A Reflective Essay

By Elizabeth Gorny-Wegrzyn and Beth Perry

Chapter Two explores the literature on educators that employ kindness as an approach to pedagogy in higher education. Through a series of reflections, we then considered how educators using a teaching philosophy guided by a PofK influenced learners' lives, enhanced their social consciousness, and facilitated meaningful learning. In sum, the literature revealed that a teaching philosophy based on a PofK is a common approach used by inspiring educators. Further, this teaching philosophy positively influences students, their learning environments, their educational achievements, and engages them to reflect on issues of social justice. A PofK also results in increased career fulfillment for teachers. Our reflections provide examples of these conclusions.

Chapter Objectives

After completing chapter two the reader will be able to

- Define a pedagogy of kindness (PofK)
- Understand how kindness can be used effectively as an approach to pedagogy in higher education
- Describe the links between a PofK and successful teaching and learning

Introduction

Plato wrote, "Do not train a child to learn by force or harshness; but direct them to it by what amuses their minds, so that you may be better able to discover with accuracy the peculiar bent of the genius of each" (Edberg, 2020). Throughout history, philosophers, academics, and researchers have deliberated about the purpose of education, its practices, and its underlying philosophical ideals (Siegel, 2010). Educational issues considered and debated since ancient times include the educational rights of learners and of society as a whole; the essential and desired curricula considering ethical, social, and political considerations; and the attributes and responsibilities of educators, including what teaching philosophies and strategies they should employ (Serbati et al., 2020; Siegel, 2010).

Presently, there still exists a social structure in higher teaching institutions that can be oppressive, paternalistic, and domineering (Breuing, 2011). This construct creates unequal power distribution in the teacher-student dyad. The educator can be the oppressor and the learner the oppressed, in that the teacher has the authority and the power and the student has none (Breuing, 2011; Giroux, 1997; Thomas, 2019; Weiler, 2001). This hierarchal structure of power, where the learner is dependent on the teacher, weakens social consciousness and undermines necessary social change (in terms of equality in race, gender, class, age, religion, and culture) (Breuing, 2011). To counter this unequal distribution of power, theorists expound on pedagogies that can help equalize these differentials, enabling learners to think independently and have a voice of their own.

Some theorists and academics endorse the concepts of critical pedagogy, which aims to support a world that is more socially just (Breuing, 2011; Giroux, 1997). Critical pedagogy is student-centered, politically oriented to social equality and change, includes practical experiences both inside and outside of the classroom adjoined to theory and is empowering and emancipatory for students of diverse backgrounds and life experiences (Breuing, 2011; Giroux, 1997). Other theorists espouse pedagogies based on hope (hooks, 2003). In her book, *Teaching Community: A Pedagogy of Hope*, hooks champions a pedagogy where a sense of community, kinship, and unity with others (both in the academy and in the outside world) is maintained and where students and educators can work together as equal partners in a learning environment that can expand minds and enhance social consciousness.

In our current time of struggle with matters of race, gender, and class, we need a pedagogy that can help learners from diverse cultures and backgrounds become empowered, have an active voice in their learning experiences, become more engaged with class activities and issues of social justice, and feel more worthy as students and as human beings. Many theorists believe that a PofK can meet these goals (Clegg & Rowland, 2010; Groves et al., 2015; Hativa et al., 2001; Loreman, 2011; Serbati et al., 2020; Thomas, 2019). Clegg and Rowland (2010) note that addressing kindness in higher education pedagogy may unsettle the established systems of the institution, those of "neo-liberal assumptions that place value on utility and cost above other human values" (p. 720). Yet, Clegg and Rowland (2010) also assert that kindness used in pedagogy can enhance learning environments and learner outcomes and forge an educator-student bond that commits to social justice.

In this chapter, we expound on the theme of inspiring educators, their teaching philosophies, and their influence on students' lives and success. We examine the literature related to one specific teaching philosophy, a PofK, and look at the outcomes for learners and educators when this philosophy is utilized. Specifically, we explore how outstanding educators who follow a teaching philosophy guided by a PofK influence students' academic and personal lives. We review and analyze the literature on the attributes of extraordinary educators; we also explored these educators' use of a teaching philosophy that uses kindness (as well as care, compassion, and empathy) in their pedagogy. We asked the questions, how does the use of a teaching philosophy founded on a PofK affect students' learning environments, and does this philosophy help improve academic outcomes and increase social consciousness for learners? Finally, we included a series of personal reflections (from both an educator's and student's point of view). The student reflections focus on experiences with exceptional educators who used kindness in their pedagogy and how these experiences touched and changed the student's life and learning. Reflections from an educator who follows this teaching philosophy provide additional answers to the questions posed.

Defining a PofK and the Link to Educator Success

As noted in Chapter one, a PofK is a teaching philosophy that is guided by kindness, empathy, compassion, and care (Serbati et al., 2020). The use of kindness, which includes care, compassion, and empathy as a teaching strategy in higher education, can positively influence learning environments and learner outcomes (Clegg & Rowland, 2010). Educators who can identify with students and form strong teacher-student relationships positively impact learners' feelings of self-worth, and these educators can favourably influence learners' academic achievements (Clegg & Rowland, 2010). Moreover, kindness as a foundation for an educational relationship can also be significant as a commitment to social justice. Clegg and Rowland (2010) explain, "kindness as a public virtue, built upon a commitment to social justice, embraces critique. In educational research, the term 'critical friend' is used by action researchers to describe the relationship between co-enquirers (be they researchers or students) who share a commitment to social justice. It combines the kindness of friendship with the critique of the educator" (p. 723). The use of kindness as a pedagogical philosophy is a complicated concept that requires an instructor to significantly identify with student concerns and try to see things from their perspective. This deep understanding of each student's individual struggles as they work to grasp new ways of learning is one of the qualities found in inspirational educators (Clegg & Rowland, 2010).

Other qualities of outstanding educators include being organized, animated, and communicating with clarity and enthusiasm, but just as importantly, extraordinary instructors empathize with students and form educator-learner connections based on mutual trust and respect (Hativa et al., 2001; Serbati et al., 2020). The use of kindness as a pedagogical strategy can benefit learner outcomes because students who feel valued become more engaged and feel motivated to try harder at academic endeavors (Clegg & Rowland, 2010). As well, the use of kindness in higher education pedagogy can nurture learning environments where students feel comfortable in exchanging ideas with each other (and with the teacher) and where learners actively listen and cooperate (Magnet et al., 2014). The exchange of divergent thoughts and the freedom to voice opinions in an academic setting can foster intellectual curiosity and can help change prejudicial attitudes toward social injustices (Breuing, 2011; Magnet et al., 2014).

Current literature reveals that the most significant factor in encouraging student learning and promoting favourable learner outcomes is the development of educator-student relationships based on kindness, respect, and empathy (Khan & Armstrong, 2019). Successful and effective teaching strategies put the focus on students, improving both their learning environments and their satisfaction with learning experiences (Henard & Roseveare, 2012). Increasing student satisfaction makes learners more engaged in scholastic endeavors and thus enhances their achievement of learning outcomes (Serbati et al., 2020). In the same sense, strong academic connections and using kindness to cultivate those connections can spark students' interest and engage them to participate in discussions that may enlighten their social consciousness (Magnet et al., 2014).

The literature consistently shows that educators who work to create mutually respectful bonds with learners establish rich and satisfying learning environments that lead to positive learner outcomes (Serbati et al., 2020). A case study of two cohorts of university students (and their reflections on academic life) by Groves et al. (2015) concluded that the most significant factor positively impacting student engagement, student involvement in studies, and learner success was the educator-student relationship. Further, the students' observations in the Groves et al. study on teacher-student relationships indicated that learners appreciated instructors who were proficient, organized, and animated but placed more value on teachers who were welcoming, accessible, and who had a sincere interest in the students' personal and academic lives (2015). These qualities, which align with a PofK, are evident in the following student reflection. The educator's reflection that follows demonstrates that a PofK has mutual benefits for learners and educators.

A Student's Experience with a PofK

Here is my story.

Returning to university to pursue my Master of Nursing degree was always a dream of mine. I graduated with my Bachelor of Science in Nursing in the year 2000 and then devoted myself to my growing family and my nursing career. In the back of my mind, though, this dream quietly lived and flourished.

In 2018, when my youngest son turned 18, I decided it was time to try and attain my dream. I was filled with excitement but also with trepidation. I wondered if I could achieve my goal after being out of the academic field for 18 years. Would I be able to succeed at a higher level of learning? Would I be disciplined enough to manage a family, a home, a career, and an education? I wasn't sure, but I knew I wanted to try. I thought of the words of Johann Wolfgang von Goethe, "What is not started today is never finished tomorrow" (Edberg, 2020).

The Master of Nursing program I enrolled in was online, and the courses were self-paced. When I started my first two courses, I felt lost in all the new technology; the online conferencing, the forums, and I thought that I might fail. As well, some people discouraged me and asked why I was going back to school at my age? I knew that the initial difficulties I faced were due to rusty study habits that could be re-trained and that in time I would familiarize myself with the online format. I reflected on my decision again and finally answered with a quote by George Bernard Shaw, "You see things; and you say, 'Why?' But I dream things that never were; and I say, 'Why not?'" (Edberg, 2020).

At the beginning of my academic journey, I found the work demanding, and often time-management was a problem. My first assignment was not as successful as I had expected (not failing but not the A I hoped for), and I questioned my decision again. I thought about withdrawing from the program, but one of my instructors reached out to me and asked me to call her. The professor asked me to explain what thoughts I was trying to express and convey in my assignment. She actively listened to my answers and encouraged me with understanding. That phone call instilled new confidence and motivated me to continue to walk down the path that eventually led to my graduation. I didn't know it at the time, but I had just encountered an exceptional educator who espoused a PofK.

In using a PofK as her teaching philosophy, the instructor in my story motivated me to continue my studies and made me feel valued as both a student and a human being. In allowing me to voice my opinions and thoughts actively she made the newly gained knowledge more meaningful, and as described by Giroux (1997) "emancipatory". Throughout my academic journey, I noticed that many educators I considered outstanding seemed to exude empathy, understanding, and concern and thereby inspired me academically. My educational experiences were all positive and enriching during my two years of study, yet some experiences were more inspiring than others. The factors that elevated class participation and engagement to a higher level were due to the qualities I observed in these exceptional educators. Looking back now, I realize the instructors who made the most significant impact on my life and learning (and on the lives and learning of other students) were those educators who used a PofK as their teaching philosophy. In brief, they cared.

In another instance, when I reflect on my most influential, enriching, and memorable course on the topic of leadership, I realize that the instructor (who was an inspiration to us all) formed a mutually respectful and trusting educator-learner relationship with each student in our class. Our professor had all the attributes of an outstanding educator, and she consistently conveyed a teaching philosophy founded on a PofK. She was able to identify with each student and was able to meet each learner's unique needs in a compassionate and individualized approach.

Denial (2019) and Serbati et al. (2020) describe exceptional educators as those who have a passion for teaching, empathy toward students, and who feel that students' contributions to the development of teaching strategies are valuable and beneficial. Exemplary teachers are also knowledgeable about their subject matter and use innovative and creative teaching methods to engage students and capture their attention (Hativa et al., 2001; Khan & Armstrong, 2019). Outstanding educators can identify with students and understand and better meet their individual and diverse needs (Loreman, 2011). Inspiring teachers help build an "intellectual community" and foster a learning environment of open communication and collaboration to help stimulate thoughts on social justice (Magnet et al., 2014). As well, exceptional teachers can adapt to existing challenges in higher education, such as technological advancements in teaching methods, movement from a traditional to online learning milieu, and increasingly diverse student populations (Contact North, 2015; Henard & Roseveare, 2012).

Our instructor in the leadership class mentioned above exemplified the qualities of an extraordinary educator who abided by a PofK. At that time, not being aware of kindness as a strategy in pedagogy, I could not articulate these thoughts. Now, on reflection, I understand why the instructor and the course were so exceptional. Our learning activities were inspiring, innovative, and thought-provoking. The class debates and dialogues were always stimulating and engaging. Every student participated with enthusiasm. We were encouraged and gently guided by our instructor to voice our opinions, thoughts, and feelings and reflect on personal experiences and apply them to our discussions. As learners, we sometimes had different viewpoints as we came from diverse backgrounds and had different life experiences. Yet, our teacher made each one of us feel that our opinions were valid and important. Through these discussions, we built connections and learned to collaborate with others.

Other instructional activities stirred our emotions and helped us achieve affective domain learning outcomes. We explored photos, videos, and inspirational quotes related to the course themes in terms of what they meant to us and our work and personal experiences. We were encouraged to explore our feelings, attitudes, biases, and values. Every sense was stimulated and engaged through these activities, and that made the class a satisfying and enriching experience. As the literature revealed, and demonstrated in this class, strong educator-learner relationships and challenging learning environments lead to increased student engagement, increased insights into social injustices, and improved learner outcomes. The students in this class strived harder and accomplished more due to the teacher's encouragement and validation that our thoughts were important and valuable. The sharing of thoughts and ideas, many different from our own, enabled us to understand our differences and to raise our awareness of social injustice. The instructor's PofK was the foundation of her, and our, success.

An Educator's Reflection on a PofK

As children we are all taught to be kind. It is the Golden Rule, "Do unto others as you would have them do unto you" (Puka, 2020). Kindness has roots in religion, sociology, philosophy, and psychology but does it have a place in education? Values associated with the Golden Rule such as empathy and caring are considered attributes of "good" people but are they appropriate and useful values of exemplary educators? These are questions I have asked myself throughout my career as an academic.

Kindness is defined as "the quality of being generous, helpful, and caring about other people, or an act showing this quality" (Cambridge University Press, n.d.). When we become educators, we are counselled that we must be fair, well-prepared, credible, and scholarly but being kind or empathic toward learners is seldom mentioned. Specifically, I was encouraged to maintain professional distance from students and to be serious and even strict especially during the initial classes in a semester. The rational for presenting with this demeanor was to "keep students from taking advantage of me" and to ensure that I maintained discipline and order in the classroom. Being "kind" was considered a sign of weakness.

As I proceeded through my almost 30-year career teaching in-person, blended, and online classes in higher education institutions I began to question this advice. I read about the "pedagogy of kindness" and the "pedagogy of care" and I realized what an essential role the educator's values play in the student experience. Willard (1929) was an early believer in the role of kindness in successful teaching and learning and Arnold (2005) specified the value of empathy in the form of empathetic intelligence as part of a pedagogy of kindness. Gradually I began to understand that being *kind* was not the same as being *nice*. Sometimes being kind required me to confront learners, challenge their viewpoints, push them to work harder, or to have difficult conversations with them.

In discussing the evolution of a PofK in higher education Magnet et al. (2014) note that kindness has traditionally been feminized and devalued. These same authors assert that being kind, as a pedagogical strategy, can eliminate dominance, oppression, and competition in the academy (Magnet et al., 2014) facilitating justice and a sense of community (Palahicky, et al, 2019). Loreman (2011) frames this approach to teaching as love which includes kindness, empathy, intimacy, and bonding, sacrifice and forgiveness, and acceptance and community.

Through various experiences with students (and considerable self-reflection), I learned that an educator's values impact student performance and therefore specific values, such as those that are part of a PofK, are essential to teaching success (Palahicky, et al, 2019). What follows is the story of one experience with a student that has impacted my teaching philosophy profoundly.

41

An early formative experience with a nursing student I will call Jasmine started me on the path of integrating kindness into my practice. Jasmine was a quiet learner, always attending class but rarely speaking up to answer or ask questions. She always seemed somewhat preoccupied and left the classroom the instant class was over without socializing with the other students. I found myself concerned about her state of well-being and as the term progressed her physical appearance became increasingly disheveled and the preoccupation and vacant glances out the window during class happened more often. As my concern for Jasmine grew, I felt a need to reach out to her to see if she needed help, yet I held back as my colleagues all warned again "getting involved" in a student's personal life. Yet her personal situation seemed to be negatively impacting her academic performance, so I decided to act.

The next day in class Jasmine appeared agitated and even more aloof and I couldn't resist any longer. I slipped her a tiny yellow sticky note that said, "if you need to talk, I am here for you." Although I waited Jasmine didn't come to me after class to pour out her heart as I had anticipated. She continued to come to class, finished the term, and passed the course. On the last day of our class she dropped an envelope on my desk. I opened it after everyone had departed. Inside the envelope was my little yellow sticky note and under my words "if you need to talk, I am here for you" Jasmine had written "thanks for caring, it made all the difference." I still have that sticky note in my box of special teaching memories.

Jasmine taught me much about how a PofK can lift a struggling learner so that that person can keep pursuing their academic goals. She also taught me that acts of kindness and empathy do not necessarily have to be overly time-consuming, intense, or "big" overtures. Kindness is often most intensely experienced through seemingly tiny gestures rendered with sincerity. Finally, the experience with Jasmine taught me that a pedagogy framed in kindness has positive effects on learners, but it equally has positive impacts on educators. A PofK has mutual benefits. I may have helped Jasmine with my small act of kindness and a willingness to be open to her sharing her worries and circumstances with me, but she equally impacted me in a positive way. As an educator knowing that I can care about students and rather than losing control of the discipline of the classroom I can enhance their learning experience and support them to succeed gives me intense career fulfillment. It also motivates me to continue to strive to be the best educator I can be.

Conclusion

This chapter examined how inspirational educators who adopt the use of kindness (including care, empathy, and compassion) in their pedagogy engage and motivate students to try harder in their academic efforts leading to positive student outcomes (Serbati et al., 2020). The literature consistently shows that extraordinary instructors who espouse a teaching philosophy founded on a PofK make a significant impact on students' lives and learning achievements (Clegg & Rowland, 2010; Groves et al., 2015; Serbati et al., 2020; Thomas, 2019). These exceptional teachers understand the unique needs of students from diverse backgrounds and cultivate learning environments that promote a sense of community and partnership (Clegg & Rowland, 2010; Magnet et al., 2014). Through the reflections of a student and an educator on the use of kindness in pedagogy, we realize that learners who encounter educators abiding by this teaching philosophy are fortunate. Not only do these students potentially have better learning outcomes, but their academic experiences are also enhanced, and their personal lives may be made richer. Extraordinary educators who make learners feel valued increase the possibility of academic success while reinforcing students' worth as human beings. Inspirational educators also encourage sharing diverse thoughts, opinions, life experiences, and values and thereby advance reflection on social justice (Clegg & Rowland, 2010; Magnet et al., 2014). Kindness is a quality in instructors that is not always encouraged by institutional administrators and may be criticized as too emotional and not rigorous enough for academia (Clegg & Rowland, 2010). Yet, as demonstrated in the reflections, this teaching approach can have profoundly positive effects on learners and educators. We argue that kindness can and should play a valuable role in pedagogy in higher education because it can positively influence learner environments, learning outcomes, teaching success, and promote discourse on social justice. Encouraging a pedagogy of kindness is much more that being kind – it is a pedagogy that challenges learners to see beyond their existing world views to appreciate and value self and others. It helps build resilience and confidence in students making them better citizens and more compassionate human beings. Finally, enacting a pedagogy based on values of caring helps educators inspire and be inspired in return.

References

Arnold, R. (2005). *Empathic intelligence: Teaching, learning, relating.* UNSW Press.

Breuing, M. (2011). Problematizing critical pedagogy. *International Journal of Critical Pedagogy, 3*(3), 1-23. https://www.marybreunig.com/assets/files/Problematizing%20Critical%2 0Pedagogy.pdf

Cambridge University Press. (n.d.). Kindness. In Cambridge Dictionary. *Cambridge University Press.* https://dictionary.cambridge.org/dictionary/english/kindness

Clegg, S., & Rowland, S. (2010). Kindness in pedagogical practice and academic life. *British Journal of Sociology of Education, 31*(6), 719-735. http://www.jstor.org/stable/25758494

Contact North. (2015). *The future of higher education: A Canadian view.* https://teachonline.ca/sites/default/files/pdfs/perspective_on_the_future_o f_higher_education.pdf

Denial, C. (2019, August 15). *A pedagogy of kindness.* https://hybridpedagogy.org/pedagogy-of-kindness/

Edberg, H. (2020, August 11). 55 inspiring quotes on dreams (and on making them real*). The Positivityblog.* https://www.positivityblog.com/quotes-on-dreams/

Edberg, H. (2020). 80 inspirational education quotes for students and teachers. *The Positivityblog.* https://www.positivityblog.com/quotes-on-education/

Giroux, H. (1997). *Pedagogy and the politics of hope.* CA, USA: Westview Press.

Groves, M., Sellars, C., Smith, J., & Barber, A. (2015). Factors affecting student engagement: A case study examining two cohorts of students attending a post-1992 University in the United Kingdom. *International Journal of Higher Education. 4*(2). http://dx.doi.org/10.5430/ijhe.v4n2p27

Hativa, N., Barak, R., & Simhi, E. (2001). Exemplary university teachers: Knowledge and beliefs regarding effective teaching dimensions and strategies. *The Journal of Higher Education, 72*(6), 699-729. http://www.jstor.org/stable/2672900

Henard, F., & Roseveare, D. (2012). *Fostering quality teaching in higher education: Policies and practices*. Paris: OECD. https://www.oecd.org/education/imhe/QT%20policies%20and%20practic es.pdf

hooks, b. (2003). *Teaching community: A pedagogy of hope*. New York: Routledge

Khan, S., & Armstrong, A. (2019). Math-a-polka: Mathematics as a place of loving kindness. *Journal of the Canadian Association for Curriculum Studies, 17*(1), 1-12. https://jcacs.journals.yorku.ca/index.php/jcacs/article/viewFile/40441/364 19

Loreman, T. (2011) Kindness and empathy in pedagogy. In Love as Pedagogy. *SensePublishers*. https://doi.org/10.1007/978-94-6091-484-3_2

Magnet, S., Mason, C., & Trevenen, K. (2014). Feminism, pedagogy, and the politics of kindness. *Feminist Teacher, 25*(1), 1-22. http://www.jstor.org/stable/10.5406/femteacher.25.1.0001

Palahicky, S., DesBiens, D., Jeffery, K., & Stuart Webster, K. (2019). Pedagogical values in online and blended learning environment in higher education. In J. Keengwe (Ed.) *Handbook of Research on Blended Learning Pedagogies and Professional Development in Higher Education* (pp. 79-101). DOI: 10.4018/978-1-5225-5557-5.ch005

Puka, B. (2020). Golden rule. *The Internet encyclopedia of philosophy*. https://iep.utm.edu/goldrule/

Serbati, A., Aquario, D., Da Re, L., Paccagnella, O., & Felisatti, E. (2020). Exploring good teaching practices and needs for improvement: Implications for staff development. *Journal of Educational, Cultural and Psychological Studies (ECPS Journal), 0*(21), 43-64. https://doi.org/10.7358/ecps-2020-021-serb

Siegel, H. (2010). Introduction: Philosophy of education and philosophy. *The Oxford Handbook of Philosophy of Education*. https://www.oxfordhandbooks.com/view/10.1093/oxfordhb/97801953128 81.001.0001/oxfordhb-9780195312881-e-001

Thomas, W. (2019, August 23). *Pedagogy of care*. https://willt486.github.io/teaching/2019/08/23/pedagogy-of-care/

Weiler, K. (Ed.). (2001). *Feminist engagements: Reading, resisting, and revisioning male theorists in education and cultural studies*. New York: Routledge

Willard, E.B. (1929). Kindness as a factor in pedagogy. *Journal of Education, 110*(7), 151–153. https://doi.org/10.1177/002205742911000704

Chapter Three:

The Pedagogy of Kindness through the Lens of Deep, Holistic Learning

By Colleen M. Stanton

Chapter Three connects my experiences using a pedagogy of kindness (PofK) while teaching and learning in the Master of Nursing and Health Studies Program, Athabasca University, with my doctoral research on A Health Promoting Continuous Learning Sustainable Education System (Stanton, 2014).

As you read this chapter, take some time to reflect on how the PofK is interwoven and entwined into creating health-promoting, continuous learning, sustainable education systems. I envision a purple thread weaving its way through the discussion on the three system environments and the reflective framework in my research. This colour comes to mind because purple makes me think of kindness, compassion, creativity, peace, deep meaning, purpose, and consciousness in life. Choose any colour of thread that comes to mind for you. I see the PofK philosophy and theories of learning, flowing through and enhancing a health-promoting, continuous learning, sustainable education system.

The research foundational of this chapter included over 70 key informant interviews with professionals. These professionals included: exemplary elementary and secondary school teachers, principals, and education system leaders, as well as recognized leaders who worked collaboratively with organizations such as the United Nations, the World Health Organization, UNESCO, and other universities. These 70 individuals shared their views on caring for each other, caring for the world, improving health, enhancing global awareness, and raising collective consciousness. The study revealed how we could work together more collaboratively in organizations and the global environment. It also uncovered the importance of leadership, learning, and interrelatedness in creating this increasing complexity and consciousness. The basis of their beliefs, insights, and values aligns with the PofK.

The major contribution of this chapter will be to enhance our understanding of the connections between the PofK and a health-promoting, continuous learning, sustainable education system. We experience how using a PofK enhances deep, holistic learning, which is foundational to achieving highly effective education systems. Effective educational systems, in turn, provide learning environments where a PofK can be enacted. Further, the chapter advances a compelling rationale for integrating the PofK into our formal teaching and learning. A reflective learning framework for self-assessment and reflection on our complexity and consciousness is also presented.

Chapter Objectives

After completing Chapter Three the reader will be able to

- Describe a health promoting, continuous learning, sustainable education system

- Link the PofK to a health promoting, continuous learning, sustainable education system

- Appreciate how utilizing the PofK in higher education strengthens our understanding and appreciation of complexity and consciousness

Context for the Pedagogy of Kindness

As evidenced in the literature and other chapters of this book, the PofK is foundational to collaborative, engaging approaches for educators and adult learners. Comprehensive research now considers practicing kindness a global movement (World of Kindness Movement, 1997). Many skilled educators view a PofK as integral to effective graduate teaching and learning.

A PofK does more than enhance educational success: it inspires learners to appreciate and value themselves and others. A PofK "helps build resilience and confidence in students making them better citizens and more compassionate human beings" (Gorny-Wegrzyn & Perry, 2021, para. Conclusion). Embracing a PofK as a teaching philosophy "encourages students and educators to thrive academically and as human beings" (Gorny-Wegrzyn & Perry, 2021, p. 8).

Kindness is a broad concept and is often used interchangeably with words like care, compassion, and empathy, which in turn encapsulate other concepts such as empathy, courtesy, helpfulness, thoughtfulness, and tolerance. Kindness encourages an appreciation of approaches such as health promotion, continuous learning, and sustainable education systems. These approaches embody diversity, sharing of power and control, stimulation of diverse opinions and values, critical and reflective thinking, mindfulness, well-being, collaboration, resilience, and the creation of engaging learning environments. Covey (2006) found in his extensive research that "the motive that inspires the greatest trust is genuine caring – caring about people, caring about purposes, caring about the quality of what you do, caring about society as a whole" (p. 26)

If we think about ways to become more effective educators, we often think of what we know about kindness as a foundation of our teaching approaches – and we all know how essential this is (Gorny-Wegrzyn & Perry, 2021, pp. 3-10). As online education becomes more common at graduate and undergraduate levels, reflective educators seek practices that successfully convey PofK in this milieu. Educators challenged with moving from the face-to-face to the online education environment often ask themselves, *What can I do to refine and extend what I know about practicing kindness as classes move online?* Initially, many educators struggle with maintaining humanity in their teaching (and all the associated values like caring, compassion, and kindness) when teaching shifts to a more potentially impersonal technological platform – the computer.

Yet, many learners (and teachers) seem to value the human connection that is often part of the in-class educational experience. We know this human connection is important because students report how positive it is to be touched by kindness and to know that their teachers and classmates are "real" people (Garrison, 2017). In turn, educators who live a PofK have enhanced career satisfaction and professional fulfillment (Taggart, 2015).

Introduction to Health Promoting, Continuous Learning, Sustainable Education Systems

In the health promotion field, scholars and practitioners are developing a deeper and more complex understanding of what creates health and how it can be generated in large systems. The PofK potentially helps promote health in humans as it focuses on the well-being of multiple aspects of people, including emotional and psychological health.

Further, human health is intertwined with the health of organizations, communities, and ecosystems. We can build on our collective consciousness through synergy to address large-scale and complex systems change. Undertaking this change can create healthier, more sustainable individuals, organizations, and global communities by working more closely across diverse sectors and disciplines, particularly with professionals in the education system.

The setting for the study described in this chapter was an education system (school district) in Ontario where there had been transformational system change. This system-level change was achieved by creating collaborative and innovative learning environments through distributed/shared leadership, capacity building, and networking. This qualitative study drew on an ecological, holistic systems approach. Semi-structured interviews were conducted with teachers, principals, and district leaders and analyzed using purposive thematic analysis. Additionally, transcripts of dialogue with several experts in systems theory, systems thinking, and change became part of the data.

Among the many findings from this study, three are particularly relevant to describing the links between PofK and deep holistic learning. Specifically, a) three system environments that influence health, well-being, and sustainability and b) a reflective framework and five levels of complexity and consciousness of health, well-being, and sustainability. The following sections frame how the PofK underpins these findings.

Three System Environments

Three system environments that most significantly influenced the health, well-being and sustainability of individuals and organizations were identified. These system environments are leadership (shared/distributed), a culture of continuous learning, and the interrelatedness of work and life.

System Environment One: Leadership (Shared/Distributed)

Leadership is defined as the process of influencing thinking, attitudes, and activities towards some goal: a capacity in the human community to shape its future; and the process of facilitating individual and collective efforts to accomplish shared objectives (modified from Senge 1990; Yukl, 2006) (as cited in Stanton, 2014, p. xiv).

Health-promoting leadership draws on higher-order levels of distributed/shared leadership, integrates empowerment, involves authentic sharing of power and control, encourages meaningful input into decision-making, promotes authenticity, is based on trust and collaboration, and creates an interactive influence process where leadership is broadly distributed/shared (Stanton, 2014, p. xv).

There is an explicit alignment between these features of health-promoting leadership and principles of PofK. For example, authentic sharing of power, control, and influence in educational relationships increases the empowerment, trust, and optimism in learners (Arneson & Eckberg, 2005). A PofK embraces a student-centred attitude in which these approaches to leadership are central. Increased participation in meaningful decision-making, evidenced by improved feedback loops and opportunities to influence, are elements of health-promoting leadership that also are congruent with the student-focused approaches of a PofK (Eriksson, 2011). Further, a culture of collaboration and community building based on trust, shared meaning and purpose, connectedness, and interdependence helps enhance self and collective efficacy and diversity that are goals of enacting a PofK and aspects of shared leadership (Moye & Henkin, 2006; RNAO, 2013).

Our understanding and appreciation of leadership are evolving. We are moving from more hierarchical approaches and models to more collaborative, synergistic, and emergent approaches (i.e., transformational leadership, authentic leadership, servant leadership, and democratic leadership). These more contemporary approaches are constantly developing as we learn how to work and learn together. Leadership is a synergistic process, and effective leadership creates new approaches, ideas, and resources. It brings together diverse worldviews, values, and understandings. When we all come together, we create a new view of reality. We find solutions, generate new resources and learn together. Pedagogues who embrace the PofK also value these outcomes for the educational experience.

Shared leadership encourages people to learn, grow, adapt, and develop as individuals, teams, and a society. Leaders and educators who encourage people to speak up, have diverse opinions and ideas and share their various worldviews align with the PofK. We are beginning to see this happening on a global basis as people become more confident in voicing their opinions, sharing their diverse worldviews, and paying more attention to social justice and equity.

Key informants in the study explained the importance of leaders being respectful, caring, and generous with their time and energy. Leaders must also encourage others to take on diverse leadership roles to facilitate continued learning and growth throughout their lives. These leaders also appreciate that people have a deep meaning and purpose in life, have family lives, and want to be treated with respect and compassion (Stanton, 2014). The study findings also revealed the importance of leaders being genuine, authentic, listening, and willing to share power and control. Leaders who embrace an approach compatible with the PofK believe that appreciation of the human spirit, and respect for all of life, engage the passion and inner motivation of people, and this allows emergent qualities, diverse gifts, and healthy relationships to flourish (Stanton, 2014).

When describing the shared/distributed leadership, one respondent in the study said, "It is the kind of leadership that finds time to sit and listen, encourage and support, sees the strengths in others...There are ups and downs in people's lives...so number one for me is being empathetic and compassionate" (Stanton 2014, p. 107). Another leader said, "It is words like empathetic, caring, integrity, passion, drive, determination, respect, responsibility. It is those words that you must assume first before you can expect anyone else to assume them" (Stanton 2014, p. 108). Finally, asked about shared leadership, a participant replied, "Leadership is about being fully human and humane and vulnerable, but some people see this as a weakness. They still think leadership is about yielding lofty power and position over others and telling people what to do…. The leaders that emulate this honesty and vulnerability and see it as a strength, have transparent discussions and dialogue" (Stanton, 2014, p. 111).

There are clear links between educators who enact a PofK and leaders who live shared/distributed leadership. Educators who embrace a PofK lead in a manner congruent with these principles and experience the outcomes reported by study participants. By sharing power and decision-making with learners, educators who follow a PofK "cause people to feel like they are important. This shows respect for people's ideas and builds on their inner motivation" (Stanton, 2014, p. 113). As we evolve as educators, we begin to more fully appreciate our interrelatedness with others and see that we have a responsibility to care for each other. Leaders who show empathy and behave compassionately with those who experience loss and grief can share their experiences and inner selves with others in an appropriate manner (Stanton 2014, p. 109). When leaders and educators do these things, they create learning and working environments where others feel safe, find a sense of community, experience comfort, and allow everyone to flourish (Stanton 2014, p. 113).

Educators who abide by a PofK convincingly endorse approaches that involve sharing, empowering, and adapting. These dimensions are best supported through a culture of trust and optimism and are kind and show care, compassion, empathy, and tolerance. A culture of distributed/shared leadership is kind. It is through kindness that students and employees grow and evolve.

System Environment Two: Culture of Continuous Learning

A culture of continuous learning is defined as an environment where learners continue to recognize priorities, values, and their personal vision of how they want to live and work; where growth and development are an embedded way of thinking, behaving and working; and where individuals are open to feedback and to making ongoing adjustments based on that feedback (Argyris,1977; Senge, 1990: Stanton, 2014).

A critical aspect of learning is our ability to learn at a deep level: to increase our capacity for double-loop and generative learning and to develop an understanding of our mental models, hidden assumptions, and worldviews (Stanton, 2014). Stimulation of new ideas, creativity, and our ability to address complex issues can also be considered elements of optimum learning for individuals and organizations.

Essential aspects of continuous learning are also integral to and woven into the PofK. For example, a culture of continuous learning is built on adaptability, creativity, a sense of coherence, and valuing diversity (Antonovky, 1996; Bandura, 1997; Cannon & Edmonson, 2004). Through continuous learning, we can develop an increased capacity to adapt to change and to generate new learning (Antonovsky & Sage, 2001; Bandura, 1997). Further, continuous learning draws on individual strengths and capacities and internal strengths of creativity, knowledge, and wisdom (Stanton, 2014, p. 21). Finally, effective learning "increases individuals' sense of power over their own lives" (Feinstein, 2002, p. 9).

A culture of continuous learning is based on collaboration to learn from each other, share diverse worldviews, and achieve shared goals. In true collaboration, we appreciate that no one person knows all the answers and that together we can learn from our interactions, experiences, families, workplaces, and each other. Eventually, those who achieve a culture of continuous learning come to a much deeper and more complex appreciation of learning. Educators who enact the principles of a PofK are well-positioned through establishing collaborative opportunities to harvest the positive outcome a culture of continuous learning provides.

A PofK helps learners to feel secure and safe in the learning environment. By feeling safe and secure, students can appreciate diverse ways of thinking and seeing the world. As Stanton noted, "Insecure people have more difficulty with diversity and different opinions and ideas. The more secure and healthy we are, the more we appreciate and even enjoy diverse ideas, opinions and ways of doing things. We can learn so much from others" (2014. p.129).

Evidence-based research has long affirmed that a culture of continuous learning promotes growth in almost every environment (Chanani & Wibowo, 2019). Researchers strongly endorse a culture of learning which exemplifies an increased capacity to adapt to change and generate new learning. They promote being able to take risks, be creative, learn from our mistakes, and develop an increased sense of personal control over our lives (Chanani & Wibowo, 2019). Together these contribute to a sense of meaning, purpose, and connectedness with colleagues and the broader world environment.

Key informants emphasized the importance of learning together, collaborating, appreciating diverse ways of thinking and seeing, being creative, tapping into their intuitive capacities, and connecting physical and emotional health and well-being (Stanton, 2014). Learning to build resilience was seen as being essential. It is only through having a strong culture of learning that making a larger contribution to education and improving the world seems possible.

These levels of engagement within a culture of learning are possible through engaging enthusiastically through a PofK. Again, we can see how the deep aspects of learning and creating a culture of continuous learning that focuses on innovation are woven into the PofK.

System Environment Three: Interrelatedness of Work and Life

Interrelatedness is defined as "a mutual or reciprocal relationship" (Stanton, 2014, p. xiv). Primary aspects of interrelatedness in work and life are also integral to and woven into the PofK. Interrelatedness has been studied for many years in the context of ecology and the development of human consciousness. Several theorists have explained that a sense of interrelatedness, spirituality, or connection to the greater whole is crucial to address the most complex problems we face (Hargreaves & Fink, 2006; Suzuki, 1997). Beatson asserts, "A certain level of consciousness is required to be able to conceptually perceive the interrelated nature of life" (2007, p. 18). Capra (2011) explained that our consciousness expands as we become more conscious and complex, and as a result, we develop higher levels of compassion and empathy. The Dali Lama (1998) also asserts that being compassionate requires a certain amount of consciousness.

Interrelatedness links to many of the foundational underpinnings of the PofK such as empathy, forgiveness, and other deep human spirit qualities. This process includes developing a greater contextual appreciation of being part of something larger than ourselves. An outcome of learning for an educator who practices a PofK can incorporate an increased awareness of their inner motivations, values, strengths, and weaknesses (Stanton, 2014, p. 149). In time learners and educators who live the values of a PofK can "start to imagine humanity is one and become aware that discrepancies and inequalities have to be addressed and diversity has to be celebrated. The result is a culture of well-being. A vision that says we are all interconnected guides our work and learning" (2014, p. 156). Another outcome of learning in an environment where a PofK is the mode of teaching and learning is that learners report becoming more caring and compassionate, that they had the urge to do something, to be of service, and to make a contribution to education and to improving the world (Staton, 2014, p. 156).

A Reflective Framework: Five Levels of Complexity and Consciousness Gaining an Appreciation of the Complexity and Consciousness of Life

While there are five levels of complexity and consciousness in this reflective framework, it is really a spiral. We go up and down and move back and forth throughout this spiral all our lives. We are not stagnant, and if we learn and grow, we can move up the spiral and become more highly complex and conscious. This discussion focuses on the top three levels of the framework: social systems, learning systems, and living systems (Stanton, 2014). See Figure 2. As we move through these systems, our complexity and consciousness are enhanced.

Figure 2.

Reflective framework: Five levels of complexity and consciousness of health, well-being, and sustainability (modified) (Stanton, 2014).

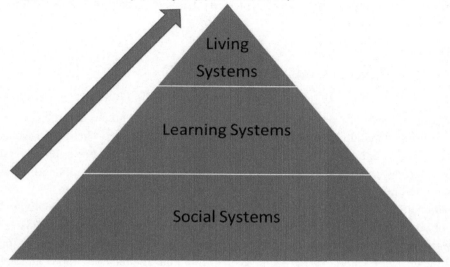

Level 3: Social Systems

Social systems promote self-esteem, social/emotional well-being, belonging, sharing, and the development of healthy, authentic, caring relationships (Stanton, 2014, pp. 26, 35). In social systems, experiences like cooperation, adaptive learning, and openness are encouraged. Organizationally, individuals in this phase of learning create a shared vision and values and gain an appreciation of interrelatedness with others (Stanton, 2014, pp. 36, 37). Educators at level 3, recognize balance, resilience, and renewal as important ongoing processes in effective learning (Stanton, 2014, pp. 6, 24, 41).

Level 4: Learning Systems

Learning systems are more self-organizing, generative, and emergent (Stanton, 2014, pp. 6-7,42-43). In this phase, educators promote an appreciation of diverse values and worldviews. There is a growing capacity for synergy and emergence (Stanton, 2014, p. 6). Higher levels of tension related to diversity develop higher levels of social consciousness (Stanton, 2014, p. 37). Educators appreciate greater diversity, openness, distinct ways of knowing, and emergence. Empathy develops as an emergent property between Levels 4 and 5 (Stanton, 2014, p. 44).

Level 5: Living Systems

During the living systems phase, people develop a greater appreciation of long-term sustainability approaches to health and well-being. These approaches are holistic and tap into the synergy of the whole. They build on diverse perspectives and reflect complexity, ambiguity, and continuous change. They promote creativity, innovation, and emergence. These approaches to long-term sustainable well-being appreciate diverse ways of knowing (spiritual, ecological, global) (Stanton, 2014, pp. 45-48). People promote higher levels of complexity/consciousness and higher levels of differentiation/integration in this top-level stage (Stanton, 2014, pp. 26). In this phase, educators appreciate and promote generative, transformational change; embrace ambiguity and unknowingness; and are committed to an inclusive vision and the common good (Stanton, 2014, p. 36). There is an appreciation of consciousness as spiritual, global, and ecological. As well, educators use terms such as reflective consciousness (Stanton, 2014, p. 6), complexity consciousness (Stanton, 2014, p. 27), social consciousness (Stanton, 2014, p. 37), and empathic consciousness (Stanton, 2014, p. 44). Those who reach this level live their beliefs.

Application of the Systems to the Pedagogy of Kindness

Most people would see the PofK from the perspective of social systems (Level 3). From this perspective, people are trying to get along and work together in collaboration. People appreciate each other, care about each other, and are kind to each other. Educators acknowledge that students have competing priorities like families and work. In the class community, students and educators share their experiences, stories, and expertise as they live the PofK. They try to help each other, find ways to support each other with challenges, and reach out to others. From the perspective of *Social Systems*, meaning, purpose, and consciousness are closely interrelated to social/emotional well-being. Individuals within the phase of the social system focus on caring for others and practicing kindness.

From the perspective of learning systems (Level 4), people become more analytical and pay attention to research. People think of new ideas and creative solutions and energize each other through their unique intellectual abilities and creativity. Individuals test out new ideas and creative solutions and take risks. People are not afraid of speaking up or being different; they see the advantages of tapping into these differences. Learning through the PofK, individuals can grow into the learning systems (Level 4), and they seek to support the growth and learning of others. Individuals within the learning systems phase focus on finding new ways of integrating PofK into their teaching and learning.

In Level 5, living systems, people recognize how interrelated we are. They work together to create a better world, greater humanity, global health, and well-being. Sometimes there is a growing spiritual awareness. Level 5 is the level of greater good consciousness, global humanity, ecological awareness, and is significantly reflected in kindness, goodwill, and love of all. Those thriving in living systems realize that they cannot exist separately and that we all contribute to the whole. Kindness is recognizing that we do not exist on our own. We are interconnected to everyone and to the planet. We all need each other and are interrelated to other humans, to nature, and our planet. Level 5 individuals live kindness as it becomes fully integrated into their consciousness.

Discussion

Understanding and appreciating complex living systems is a lifelong process. Kindness is about love, caring, compassion, understanding, interrelationships, leadership, learning, change, growth, and health. It is a way of processing life. Kindness is how we support others in our lifelong journey of growth and development, increasing awareness and change. In considering the context for the PofK, it is important to remember that politeness is not the same as kindness. Being polite is saying what makes people feel good today. Being kind is doing what helps people get better tomorrow.

The research described in this chapter focused on creating living systems that are health-promoting, encourage continuous learning, and are sustainable. This overall philosophy and conceptual framework are congruent with many concepts and pillars that are identified in the PofK including, constructivism, invitational learning theory, open pedagogy, positivity, mindfulness, gratitude, arts-based pedagogy, and critical pedagogy. We are living systems that are increasing our complexity and consciousness. Through continuous learning, we are coming to a deeper understanding of how we are interrelated to the whole, and how we can work together to create greater humanity. Engaging in true diversity, whatever its form, through the lens of what we know about the PofK, will enrich a person's sense of their own meaning and purpose as they grow in increasing complexity and consciousness.

The underpinnings of the PofK are foundational underpinnings of and woven into a health-promoting, continuous learning, sustainable system. An appreciation of human goodness, kindness, and trust and the ability to care for each other and the globe significantly contribute to our health, well-being, and sustainability. Practicing the PofK helps us all to recognize that we are all leaders, and we need to share power, control, and ideas across systems. We learn that distributed/shared leadership is more appropriate for creating health-promoting, sustainable, learning systems.

Through the intersections of this study with the PofK, we learn the importance of creating learning environments that are collaborative and which encourage divergent worldviews, opinions, and values. We learn to encourage people to ask questions. We learn that by feeling empowered and developing critical thinking (through creativity and collaboration), we come to more fully recognize and appreciate the importance of meaning and purpose in our lives. We learn about the interrelatedness of complexity and consciousness that necessarily draws on mindfulness practices to support increased health and well-being.

Conclusion

Through reflecting on the PofK, we are reminded of the significant responsibilities we have as educators to continue to grow in our teaching and learning processes. As we grow and become more conscious, we find more ways to integrate mindfulness and gratitude into our teaching and learning. We see the value of creativity and innovation through various forms of arts-based pedagogy. We treat people with respect, care, and kindness, but at the same time, we challenge them to continue to grow, take risks, and innovate. The PofK merits being seen as both a global movement and an important philosophy and practice unto itself in promoting human growth.

Learning is an emerging, synergistic, integrative process. That is why learning can be seen as interwoven into the very fabric of a health-promoting, continuous learning, sustainable education system. Learning framed by a PofK appreciates people for their differences, encourages people to speak up and be themselves, recognizes how we can learn from diverse viewpoints, and supports the use of creativity and lived experience in learning. A PofK appreciates that we are moving to share power and control and that we all have our unique meaning and purpose in life that is our essence.

The PofK is a philosophy and practice that significantly influences our education environment. The PofK plays a role in developing our capacity to be kind, caring, loving human beings who are continuously learning, and contributing to creating a better world environment. Leadership based on a PofK philosophy and practice can help us work together: to create deep learning environments; collaborative shared and distributed leadership; encourage creativity; ensure respect and compassion for individuals and our broader community; value and listen carefully to diverse opinions and worldviews, and promote a deep sense of meaning and purpose that is essential for life. This philosophy is a synergistic, emergent process of increasing complexity and consciousness and a greater appreciation of our interrelatedness with all of life.

References

Antonovsky, A. (1996). The salutogenic model as a theory to guide health promotion. *Health Promotion International, 11*, 11–19.

Antonovsky, H., & Sagy, S. (2001). The development of a sense of coherence and its impact on responses on stress situations. *Journal of Social Psychology, 126*(2), 313–335.

Argyris, C. (1977). Double loop learning organizations. *Harvard Business Review*, (September–October), 115–125.

Arneson, H., & Ekberg, K. (2005). Evaluation of empowerment processes in a workplace health promotion intervention based on learning in Sweden. *Health Promotion International, 20*(4), 351–359.

Bandura, A. (1997). *Self-efficacy: The exercise of control.* W. H. Freeman.

Beatson, L. (2007). *A phenomenological study of interrelatedness and leadership for the common good* (Unpublished doctoral dissertation). Gonzaga University, Spokane, WA.

Cannon, M. D., & Edmonson, A. C. (2004). *Failing to learn and learning to fail (intelligently): How great organizations put failure to work to improve and innovate.* http://conversation-matters.typepad.com/files/edmondson---failing-to-learn-and-learning-to-fail.pdf

Capra, F. (1996). *The web of life: A new scientific understanding of living systems.* Random House.

Chanani, U. L., & Wibowo, U. B. (2019). A learning culture and continuous learning for a learning organization. *KnE Social Sciences, 2019*, 591–598.

Covey, S. (2006). *The speed of trust.* Free Press.

Eriksson, A. (2011). *Health-promoting leadership: A study of the concept and critical conditions for implementation and evaluation* (Doctoral dissertation, Nordic School of Public, Gothenburg, Sweden. http://www.nhv.se/upload/Biblioteket/Andrea%20Eriksson%20kappa.pdf

Feinstein, L. (2002). *Quantitative estimates of the social benefits of learning, 2: Health (depression and obesity)* [Wider benefits of learning research report no. 6].

http://citeseerx.ist.psu.edu/viewdoc/download?doi=10.1.1.107.6227&rep=
rep1&type=pdf

Garrison, D. R. (2017). E-Learning in the 21st Century: *A Community of Inquiry Framework for Research and Practice* (3rd edition). Routledge/Taylor and Francis.

Gorny-Wegrzyn, E. & Perry, B. (2021). Inspiring educators and a pedagogy of kindness: A reflective essay. *Creative Education, 12*(1). https://www.scirp.org/journal/paperinformation.aspx?paperid=106777

Gorny-Wegrzyn, E. (2022). *Pedagogy of kindness: Changing lives, changing the world.* Generis Publishing (under review).

Hargreaves, A., & Fink, D. (2006). *Sustainable leadership.* Jossey-Bass.

Moye, M., & Henkin, A. (2006). Exploring associations between employee empowerment and interpersonal trust in managers. *Journal of Management Development, 25*(2), 1010–1017.

RNAO (Registered Nurses' Association of Ontario). (2013, July). *Developing and sustaining nursing leadership best practice guideline* (2nd ed.). http://rnao.ca/sites/rnao-ca/files/LeadershipBPG_Booklet_Web_1.pdf

Senge, P. (1990). *The fifth discipline: The art and practice of the learning organization.* Doubleday Press.

Stanton, C. (2014) *A health promoting continuous learning sustainable education system,* Unpublished PhD Thesis. https://tspace.library.utoronto.ca/bitstream/1807/68213/1/Stanton_Colleen _M_201411_PhD_thesis.pdf

Suzuki, D. (1997). *The sacred balance: Rediscovering our place in nature.* Greystone Books.

Taggart, G. (2015). Sustaining care: cultivating mindful practice in early years professional development. Early Years: Journal of International Research & Development, 35(4), 381–393. https://0-doi-org.aupac.lib.athabascau.ca/10.1080/09575146.2015.1105200

Tension. (n.d.). In *Merriam-Webster's online dictionary and thesaurus.* http://www.merriam-webster.com/dictionary/tension

UNESCO Commission. (1996). *UNESCO's four pillars of learning.* http://www.unesco.org/delors/fourpil.htm

WHO (World Health Organization). (1986). *The Ottawa Charter for Health Promotion.*
http://www.who.int/healthpromotion/conferences/previous/ottawa/en/

Yukl, G. (2006). *Leadership in organizations.* NJ: Prentice Hall.

Chapter Four:

Art-Based Strategies: Ways to Enact a Pedagogy of Kindness and Open Pedagogy

By Beth Perry and Katherine Janzen

Chapter Objectives

After completing chapter four the reader will be able to

- Describe open pedagogy (OP)
- Demonstrate the links between OP and a PofK
- Understand how arts-based instructional strategies can enact a philosophy of OP

Introduction

Open pedagogy (OP), which uses various teaching strategies to promote collaboration, connection, diversity, and democracy, is championed by many educators. Art-based instructional strategies are beneficial approaches to enacting a philosophy of OP. The outcome of the skillful use of art-based strategies, in the pursuit of OP, in turn, supports a pedagogy of kindness (PofK). The purpose of this chapter is to describe OP and to demonstrate links between OP and PofK. Examples of art-based teaching strategies (APTs) that promote OP and PofK are described. This chapter provides educators with techniques they can use to achieve the goals of OP and PofK in various educational settings and disciplines.

Describing Open Pedagogy

No one definition of OP is evident, however, authors consistently refer to common elements when seeking to describe this educational philosophy. The critical principles of OP include empowering students and moving from teacher-centred to student-centred practices (Visser & Flynn, 2018) and power redistribution in student-teacher interactions resulting in less hierarchical relationships (Baran & AlZoubi, 2020). Further, several goals of OP include the removal of barriers around what knowledge is, how knowledge comes to be known, and how knowledge is shared and exemplified with the use and production of open educational resources (OER) and the use of public knowledge repositories (Kalir, 2020). Educators who embrace a philosophy of OP value students as collaborators, inviting them to make essential contributions to the course (i.e., making recommendations about the syllabi, learning activities, and assessments) and working with them to co-create knowledge to share for the benefit of others.

Conceptually, Jhangiani and Green (2018) consider learner empowerment as the central pedagogical premise of OP. Educators share power and control, resulting in the development of trust, which is the foundation of effective student-teacher relationships (Katz & Halpern, 2015). When educators collaborate and connect with learners, learner self-confidence is magnified. This confidence and empowerment, in turn, fuels student motivation and engagement, ultimately enhancing learning and retention of knowledge. The decentralized power in OP enhances student agency, which sequentially promotes further connectivity and reflection in a positive cycle (DeRosa & Jhangiani, 2017). (See Figure 1). The decentralization of power in the educational milieu also results in increased democracy in the learning environment (Werth & Williams, 2021). Diversity is essential to an effective OP as each learner is considered unique and valued for their uniqueness and what they bring to collaborations (Chuang, 2021).

Figure 3.

Links between Decentralized Power, Student Agency, Learning, and Connection

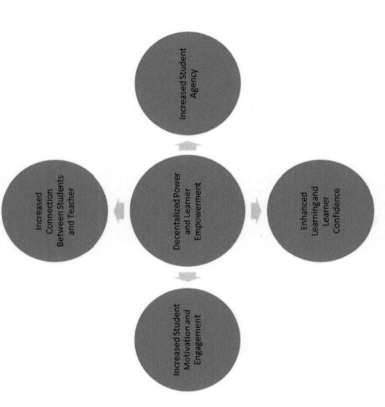

Through collaboration and connection, learners engage with teachers to co-create knowledge and demonstrate their learning through artifacts of knowledge creation (Arokiya Raj & Aram, 2019). Open pedagogical approaches result in enhanced learner motivation and engagement, in part because learning outcomes are more meaningful to students and the learning experience is more participatory (Werth & Williams, 2021). When outcomes of learning include non-disposable and reusable artifacts that can be shared openly and widely as open educational resources (OER), students get a sense that their study has utility. A project created through an open pedagogical approach has value for other than the person who created it and can be shared publicly, fostering critical thinking and self-direction (Tillinghast, 2020).

OP is consistent with constructivist learning theory, based on the view that students learn from experience and reflection (Arokiya Raj & Aram, 2019). Constructivists consider learners are self-directed, and they encourage learners to actively construct knowledge from activities, personal experiences, and reflections while teachers take the role of supporter, facilitator, and mentor (Chuang, 2021). Effective learning is active, collaborative, focused on problem-solving, and experiential rather than passive. These attributes enhance learner motivation and retention of knowledge (Chuang, 2021). In sum, the parallels between constructivist learning theory and the philosophy of OP are consistent and extensive.

OP positively impacts learners, learning, and the learning experience. How do educators enact OP? Open pedagogues not only respect the life experiences of students and value their diversity, but they also use teaching approaches that encourage learners to express their life experiences and share learning from these experiences with self and others. Hegarty (2015) lists establishing openness and trust, valuing innovation and creativity, sharing of ideas and resources, creating a sense of connected community, focusing on learner-generated content in assignments, promoting reflective practice, and utilizing peer review as approaches that enact OP in a class. Teaching strategies used by educators who aspire to OP promote collaboration, connection, diversity, and democracy in the learning environment.

Open Pedagogy and Pedagogy of Kindness

Educators who utilize a Pedagogy of Kindness (PofK) are viewed by students as; accessible, welcoming, collaborative, and respectful (Rawle, 2021). Further, educators who live a PofK form mutually beneficial relationships with learners and collaborate as equals in the teaching-learning process (Serbati et al., 2020). The PofK is framed by the principle of justice, believing people, and believing in people (Santovec, 2021). To believe people, you must first trust people. The value of trust links the PofK and OP. In both philosophies, the trust between students and educators is essential for optimal learning.

When educators believe in students, the natural outcome is collaboration (a principle of OP). Educators who believe that students bring knowledge and experiences to the learning environment that should be valued and shared will enable students to co-create knowledge. Educators who enact PofK will also encourage students to share that knowledge with others, often through non-disposable learning artifacts. Believing in students gives them the confidence to be curious and creative and to find ways to meet their own learning needs and goals (Denial, 2019). A PofK is about being empathetic to the other and open to shared power in learning relationships which parallels OP precisely.

Clegg and Rowland (2010) caution that some think kindness has no place in education and label it as sentimental and void of critical thinking. Rawle (2021) notes that critics of PofK believe that being kind is not compatible with academic success and rigour. However, a PofK is not about coddling and niceness; it is about being authentic and prioritizing compassion (Santovec, 2021). Clegg and Rowland (2010) distinguish feeling kind and kindness, saying PofK (kindness) requires academically skilled educators. Educators who live by a PofK may have hard conversations with learners, as prioritizing student learning is always the underlying goal of student-teacher interactions (Denial, 2019). Rawle (2021) concludes that educators who enact a PofK have connection, care, and compassion at the core of their teaching, which improves learning and student wellness.

In sum, a PofK supports an empathetic learning environment to individual learner needs and promotes a sense of community, collaboration, and class partnership. A PofK enables students to improve the outcomes of their academic endeavours. This teaching philosophy also supports student-centred learning, respects differences in students' backgrounds and educational goals, and helps students feel valuable and worthwhile as human beings (Serbati et al., 2020).

Finally, living a PofK is mutually beneficial for students and educators. This pedagogy allows educators to appreciate students' contributions to the educational process as respected partners, thus affording teachers career fulfillment and satisfaction (Perry & Edwards, 2019; Serbati et al., 2020).

Examples of Art-Inspired Teaching Strategies that Correlate with Open Pedagogy and A Pedagogy of Kindness

Let me start with a story. I had just returned from presenting a paper on art-based teaching strategies (APTs) at a conference in Portugal. I was to share my presentation from that conference with the faculty at my university. Sharing a presentation with faculty after attending a teaching conference was an expectation. I was nervous when presenting to my colleagues as I did not know how they would respond to my ideas. I used a lot of metaphors and analogies to help them understand APTs. Much to my delight faculty in attendance were excited not only about the concept of art-inspired strategies, but they wanted to try APTs in their classrooms. One very experienced faculty member commented, "Damn, now I have to change the way I teach!" She did not say "damn" with a negative tone. She was excited about the possibilities for students (and herself) that she saw in APTs. At times instructors hang on to familiar educational tools that worked well at one point but have become outdated. Educators using APTs are risk-takers and require courage. Introducing anything new in an academic structure can be daunting, but instructors with determination and passion for teaching can achieve it.

Many instructors found the courage to try APTs with very positive outcomes following my presentation. Instructors were excited to use this new way of engaging students. In academia, educators are often required to conform to course syllabi and pre-designed teaching outlines. However, many instructors are told what to teach but not how to teach. APTs provide instructors who strive to live OP and PofK with tools to help achieve this goal. These strategies help educators challenge traditional instructional approaches and allow them to introduce new ways of teaching and learning into their classrooms.

We have been developing, using, and studying the effects of APTs on students and instructors in the online teaching context for several years (Perry et al., 2019). We have found that these low-tech digital instructional strategies engage students and inspire educators who teach undergraduate and graduate courses online and face-to-face (Perry et al., 2019). In this section, several APTs are described as ways to incorporate OP and PofK into your teaching practice.

Arts-based instructional strategies stimulate student creativity and critical thinking and assist in achieving cognitive and social-emotional learning outcomes (Perry et al., 2019). When learner engagement is enhanced, a sense of community online develops, and interaction among class members and between students and instructors increases (Perry & Edwards, 2019). These techniques also benefit teachers as adding APTs to their teaching repertoires increases their motivation and fulfillment (Perry & Edwards, 2019).

Rawle (2021) writes that educators can create an ethos of openness and kindness by utilizing specific design principles and teaching approaches. Below we describe APTs that we have used to enact the ethos Rawle (2021) describes.

APTs and Connection

First, Rawle (2021) suggests a PofK in the classroom can be made manifest by educators who make deliberate connections with learners and facilitate student-to-student connections. Educators establishing these connections use learning activities that demonstrate to students that their personal experiences are important and of value to the class. Certain activities allow students to create knowledge as a group and facilitate student-to-student connections. Additionally, students connect with teachers and fellow students who are open and share elements of their experience and personality during learning activities. The reality of shared experiences becomes evident in some APT activities and facilitates connections.

An APT called elevator speeches provides an avenue for establishing connections and for students to feel they are important members of the class community. In 1853 Otis invented the elevator we use to move about in large city buildings (Courage, 2018). Otis also developed elevator speeches to stimulate succinct discussions between two people riding in an elevator. The challenge Otis proposed was to complete a 'pitch' speech in an elevator between the time a person first pushed the elevator button and the time the individual reached the highest floor in the building (Courage, 2018).

We used Otis' idea and created an elevator speech APT as the capstone learning activity in a leadership course in a nursing program. The students worked in groups of 4 people and created a 4-minute-long video/audio presentation (elevator speech on a course topic) that they posted on a discussion board for other students in the class to access. All students reviewed the posted elevator speeches and gave them a rating of one to four stars. The instructor tabulated the stars given each speech and held an "Oscars Night" to recognize students' achievements. The elevator speeches were very creative and used various art modalities including, graphics, dramatic oratory, music, and other art forms. The "trophies" on Oscar night (crafted by the instructor) were plastic chocolate-filled champagne glasses labelled with the winner's name and the award category. The instructor also created award certificates to accompany the trophies. Award categories included Best Video Presentation, Best Audio Presentation, Best Graphics, Best Creative Presentation, Best Music, etc. Every group received an award. The award ceremony was "advertised" in the class before the event to generate engagement and anticipation in the class community.

On the day of the award presentations, students were excited. The opportunity to be the Master of Ceremonies for the event was extended to the whole class, and one student volunteered to be the host. Students also volunteered to present the awards in a manner similar to what they had observed during the actual Academy Awards. The instructor prepared envelopes for each category that included the names of the nominees and the winner. There was palatable excitement in the classroom as the presenters read the nominees for each category. Students spontaneously added desk top drum rolls, and there was applause when students heard the names of nominees read aloud. Finally, the envelope with the awards was opened, and the winner in the category was announced. The students cheered each time for their classmates.

The students and the instructor established connections, as did the students themselves because the instructor and the entire class shared in this activity. This APT activity became a shared experience. Students had the opportunity to celebrate both their achievements and the achievements of their classmates. Students reported they appreciated the instructor's efforts to design the activity and to recognize their learning in this creative way. Beyond the shared experience of the exciting awards event, students found they achieved learning outcomes as they were required to convey their ideas concisely in their elevator speeches. In a research study, Begley (2017) found that elevator speech learning activities are " frequently singled out as the most valuable aspect of a course" (para 10). In our experience, students noted in their course evaluations that the elevator speech activity was the best APT they experienced all semester.

Second, Rawle (2021) suggests learning activities that encourage dialogue and feedback facilitate OP and PofK. Several APTs include substantial opportunities for educators and students (and groups of students) to discuss and exchange feedback. Trust emerges when students experience educators who listen to them and act on feedback. Trust is a cornerstone of both OP and PofK.

In the APT of Photovoice, dialogue and feedback are an integral part of each students' experience. Photovoice was created as a participatory-action research methodology. Researchers used photographs to elicit, bring forth, and draw out responses from participants on issues related to their health and community need (Wang & Burris, 1997). This research methodology enabled participants to reflect and effectively communicate their perceptions and insights (Wang, 1999). We took the PV research method and transformed it into a teaching strategy. Photovoice as an APT involves analysis of a purposefully selected photographic image. Either the instructor chooses a photo and presents it with an accompanying reflection question for students to respond to, or students choose an image representing some aspect of their learning or experience and share their photographic image (and their analysis) with the instructor and the class. Instructors (and classmates) provide feedback and engage in dialogue around the concepts illustrated in the photo and photo analysis.

In one example using Photovoice, nursing students beginning their clinical practicum were introduced to reflective journaling using photographic images as writing/storytelling triggers. The instructor shared a photo depicting a challenge learners face during clinical experiences. Then students used that image (and the accompanying reflection question) to stimulate their thoughts for their first journal entry. For example, the instructor shared a photo of a young nurse exhibiting signs of stress (as often students are very anxious at the onset of a clinical learning experience) accompanied by the reflection question – How do you feel on day 1 of clinical? In the weeks that followed, student selected their own images relating to an experience they had during clinical and included their chosen images with their journal reflections. Students shared their weekly journals with the instructor, who provided feedback to students individually.

The students' journals became a critical medium for communication between students and their instructor. The image-triggered reflections were often very personal, honest, and revealing, and the journals were an opportunity for the instructor to provide students with individualized encouragement and understanding. One instructor who used Photovoice to encourage students to express themselves freely in their journals noted, "student journals were imbedded with emotion and often heartfelt sharing of the joys and challenges of their clinical experiences. I responded to each student's journal entry with encouragement and wrote about the strengths and development I saw in them as they progressed through clinical. I became a primary cheerleader for students expressed in the feedback I gave them. The feedback engendered a shared sense of trust in our relationship, which developed over the semester. As the clinical rotation progressed, students often shared very personal experiences with me in their reflective journals. I was allowed to be part of their worlds, and their words and experiences became a part of mine. That trust given to me was honoured and never violated. The ATP of Photovoice became a valuable vehicle for encouraging dialogue and feedback. The students taught me so much during that semester about life and nursing. Thus, the "sage" became the student." When we use APTs to encourage dialogue (either among students in the class or between a student and the instructor) it is an opportunity for us to learn from one another, and it demonstrates to students we are genuinely interested in listening to them.

APTs Encourage Risk-Taking and Reframe Failure

Third, reframing failure is a crucial approach in OP and a PofK that can be demonstrated in APTs. Regarding reframing failure, Rawle suggests, "strive for an ethos of 'practice makes progress' rather than the traditional 'practice makes perfect' and emphasize a growth mindset" (2021). This attitude expressed by the instructor helps students practice self-compassion and focus on learning. This teaching approach also gives students the courage to take on learning challenges and expand what they currently see as their limits.

Aligning with reframing failure, one common principle of APTs is that there are no right or wrong answers (Perry & Edwards, 2019). When educators reassure students that they cannot "fail" students often summon the courage to try learning activities they might have avoided. One APT that some students could find overwhelming is Conceptual Quilting. Conceptual Quilting is usually situated at the end of a unit (or a course) as a summary activity. The idea for this activity derives from the craft of quilt-making. Learners are invited to create virtual quilts by piecing together words, ideas, metaphors, and concepts from a course (or unit in a course) that they found most personally transformational. Conceptual Quilting requires learners to reflect on what they have learned, choosing important "take away" ideas and concepts to feature in their quilts.

Conceptual quilts vary considerably from student to student, demonstrating personalization of learning and acknowledging the value of diversity. This activity is none-graded and optional. The quilts are created in a medium that can be shared electronically with the instructor and classmates. Students use various drawing software to produce their quilts, with a single PowerPoint slide being the most common. To develop conceptual quilts, learners must review course materials and reflectively interact with themselves. The quilts become pictorial representations of their reflections on their experiences with course materials, classmates, and instructors. Instructors encourage students to embrace their creative abilities in designing their quilts and reassure them that all quilts will be "perfect" because they are a unique representation of that person's experiences. In this activity, learners are freed to take risks and learn in new ways. This student-centred activity that aligns with OP and PofK is experienced as empowering by many learners.

APTs Encourage Student Choice

APTs usually include an element of choice. Rawle (2021) reminds us that including choice in course design encourages students to take ownership of their own learning. Even participating (or not) in APTs is the student's choice. The instructor presents APTs as part of a suite of learning activities designed to help students achieve a particular learning outcome. Students can select the activities that match their learning style and preferences, personalizing the educational experience.

In addition, students often make the APT their own by altering various components of the activity again to individualize their learning and make the class student-centred. For example, in many APTs, students decide in what form they will present the product of their study (i.e., a podcast, a sculpture, a drawing, a song etc.). Students who have the opportunity to choose various elements related to their learning redistribute the power in the teacher-learner relationship making it less hierarchical. These outcomes lead to OP and PofK.

APTs Promote Collaboration

Collaboration is a key feature of OP and PofK, and APTs are often designed to be collaborative events. In some instances, students and the instructor work together in a shared activity, and other times groups of students work together to create a learning artifact. For example, groups of students can collaborate to create a song about a course theme or to write a poem related to a course concept. Other times students (or students and the instructor) collaborate to craft a paper for publication or revise a course syllabus.

One example of an APT student-instructor collaboration, based on the art of letter writing/storytelling, we call A Letter to my Future Self. This activity involves learners collaborating with instructors to create a learning activity that influences learners today and in the future. In this activity, the instructor asks each student to write a letter to the person they aspire to be in five years. The instructor collects, reads, and provides feedback and encouraging comments on each letter. The letters are infused with students' hopes and dreams about the professional and person they will become. To collaborate (and reciprocate), the instructor also writes a letter to each student. The instructor speaks to the potential they see in each student, encouraging them to never give up on their dreams. After the students read the feedback in the letters from the instructor, the instructor has the students put the letters in self-addressed envelopes, which the instructor mails to them five years later. Eventually, the student receives their letter with their own early thoughts about their future lives and the reminder from their instructor that they can and will achieve their dreams.

These are just a few examples of APTs that correlate with the principles of OP and a PofK. Educators striving to enact these approaches to teaching and learning might consider how teaching strategies that utilize various forms of art such as drama, music, photography, storytelling, sculpture, poetry, or handicrafts can humanize the learning environment. In looking back to some of the key attributes of OP and PofK, including the focus on people, openness, trust, collaboration, innovation, creativity, sharing, reflection (Hegarty, 2015), student-centeredness, and empowerment (Visser & Flynn, 2018), it is evident that APTs align with many of these essential traits.

To end, we return to the story about the faculty member teaching their colleagues about APTs presented at the beginning of this section. She said, "After I gave the presentation on APTs to my colleagues I was invited to create a faculty interest group related to using APTs in the classroom. Thirteen faculty members attended our monthly gatherings and reported on how they were using APTs in their teaching. Faculty expressed that 'APTs really work' and that they had a positive impact on students." In brief, these educators found that APTs helped their students to create, learn, and share, not only with the instructor but with each other. They agreed that instructor and student experiences in the classroom were enriched using APTs. These instructors had found a means to enact OP and a PofK in their teaching, which increased their career fulfillment and benefited learners in many ways.

Conclusion

OP and a PofK are philosophies educators in many disciplines can use to enhance the student experience and increase learning. Both learners and instructors benefit when instructors use strategies that promote collaboration, connection, diversity, and democracy. The arts and APTs provide educators with ways to enact these philosophies in various learning environments (in-person, online, hybrid). Further, these approaches can be used in numerous disciplines. We encourage educators to begin by being kind to themselves, to read widely to learn from others who practice a PofK, and to observe colleagues who practice from the OP and PofK standpoint. Together we can change teaching, learning, and the world.

References

Arokiya Raj, A. P. F., & Aram, I. A. (2019). Understanding open pedagogy and designing a constructivist learning in Indian MOOCs. *2019 IEEE Learning With MOOCS (LWMOOCS), MOOCS (LWMOOCS), 2019 IEEE Learning With,* 170–173. https://doi.org/10.1109/LWMOOCS47620.2019.8939616

Begley, G. S. (2017). Using elevator speeches to develop research & communication skills in biology. *Journal of Microbiology &Biology Education, 19*(1), 19-1. https://doi.org/10.1128/jmbe.v19i1.1405

Baran, E., & AlZoubi, D. (2020). Affordances, challenges, and impact of open pedagogy: Examining students' voices. *Distance Education, 41*(2), 230-244. https://doi.org/10.1080/01587919.2020.1757409

Chuang, S. (2021). The applications of constructivist learning theory and social learning theory on adult continuous development. *Performance Improvement, 60*(3), 6. https://doi.org/10.1002/pfi.21963

Clegg, S., & S. Rowland. (2010). Kindness in pedagogical practice and academic life. *British Journal of Sociology of Education, 31*(6), 719–735.

Courage, J. (2018). *The first elevator pitch: Things we've learned, entrepreneurship.* https://blog.42courses.com/home/2018/9/3/the-first-elevator-pitch

DeRosa, R., & Jhangiani, R. S. (2017). Open pedagogy. In L. Mays (Ed.), *A guide to making open textbooks with students.* Rebus Foundation. https://press.rebus.community/makingopentextbookswithstudents/chapter/open-pedagogy

Hegarty, B. (2015). Attributes of open pedagogy: A model for using open educational resources. *Educational Technology,* 3–14. https://www.scribd.com/doc/276569994/Attributes-of-Open-Pedagogy-A-Model-for-Using-Open-Educational-Resources

Jhangiani, R. S. & Green, A. (2018). An open athenaeum: Creating an institutional home for open pedagogy. In A. Wesolek, J. Lashley, & A. Langley (Eds.), *OER: A field guide for academic librarians* (pp. 141–161). Pacific University Press.

Kalir, J. H. (2020). Social annotation enabling collaboration for open learning. *Distance Education, 41*(2), 245-260. https://doi.org/10.1080/01587919.2020.1757413

Katz, J.K., & Halpern, D.D. (2015). Can virtual museums motivate students? Toward a constructivist learning approach. *Journal of Science Education & Technology, 24*(6), 776– 788. https://0-doi-org.aupac.lib.athabascau.ca/10.1007/s10956-015-9563-7

Perry, B., & Edwards, M. (2019). Arts-based learning approaches adapted for mobile learning. *Open Praxis, 11*(3). https://openpraxis.org/index.php/OpenPraxis/article/view/967/600

Perry, B., Edwards, M., & Janzen, K. (2019). Enhancing e-learner engagement by using narrative fiction in online nursing and health disciplines courses. In C. Jarvis & P. Gouthro (Eds.). *Professional Education with Fiction Media: Imagination for Engagement and Empathy in Learning.* Springer.

Rawle, F. (2021). A pedagogy of kindness: the cornerstone for student learning and wellness. *The Campus.* https://www.timeshighereducation.com/campus/pedagogy-kindness-cornerstone-student-learning-and-wellness

Rieger, K. L., Chernomas, W. M., McMillan, D. E., & Morin, F. L. (2020). Navigating creativity within arts-based pedagogy: Implications of a constructivist grounded theory study. *Nurse Education Today, 91.* https://doi.org/10.1016/j.nedt.2020.104465

Santovec, M. L. (2021). Developing and practicing a pedagogy of kindness. *Women in Higher Education, 7,* 11. https://0-doi-org.aupac.lib.athabascau.ca/10.1002/whe.21013

Serbati, A., Aquario, D., Da Re, L., Paccagnella, O., & Felissatti, E. (2020). Exploring good teaching practices and needs for improvement: Implication for staff development. *Journal of Educational, Cultural and Psychological Studies, 21,* 43-64. https://doi.org/10.7358/ecps-2020-021-serb

Tillinghast, B. (2020). Developing an open educational resource and exploring OER-enabled pedagogy in higher education. *IAFOR Journal of Education: Technology in Education, 8*(2). https://doi.org/10.22492/ije.8.2.09

Visser, R., & Flynn, A. B. (2018). What are students' learning and experiences in an online learning tool designed for cognitive and metacognitive skill development? *Collected Essays on Learning and Teaching, 11*, 129-140. http://0-search.ebscohost.com.aupac.lib.athabascau.ca/login.aspx?direct=true&AuthType=url,ip,uid&db=eric&AN=EJ1182852&site=ehost-live

Wang, C., & Burris, M. (1997). Photovoice: Concept, methodology, and use for participatory needs assessment. *Health Education Behaviour, 24*, 369-387.

Wang, C.C. (1999). Photovoice: A participatory action research strategy applied to women's health [Electronic version]. *Journal of Women's Health, 8*(2), 185-192.

Werth, E., & Williams, K. (2021). What motivates students about open pedagogy? Motivational Regulation Through the Lens of Self-Determination Theory. *International Review of Research in Open and Distance Learning, 22*(3). https://doi.org/10.19173/irrodl.v22i3.5373

Chapter Five:

Using Positivity, Mindfulness, and Gratitude in Pedagogy

By Regan Hack

Chapter five dives into understanding how positivity, mindfulness, and gratitude are valuable tenets of the PofK and what employing them with intention (at all levels) could mean for education and beyond institutional walls. A solid understanding of how these attitudes influence people, their self-concept, their decisions in life, and their interactions with others is the first step in helping others create and curate a more positive and mindful worldview and lived experience. We start by exploring the individual concepts and expand into a description of their relevance to the PofK. The chapter concludes with the impact of intentional integration of the PofK, which is a society that promotes positivity, mindfulness, and gratitude in everyday life.

Chapter Objectives

After completing chapter five the reader will be able to

- Define positivity, positive pedagogy, mindfulness, and gratitude
- Describe strategies for implementing these concepts into teaching and learning praxis
- Reflect on the impact on society of incorporating positivity, mindfulness, and gratitude into everyday life

Introduction

"It's not our job to toughen our children up to face a cruel and heartless world. It's our job to raise children who will make the world a little less cruel and heartless." – L.R. Knost

The first step to understanding why positivity, mindfulness, and gratitude are valuable tenets of the PofK is to share what they are and why they are critical to include in teaching and learning praxis throughout the entire educational experience. A major thread of connection between the PofK and these attitudes is that they all focus on strengths; they consistently bring the positive back to primary consideration and encourage building from this positive starting point. Engaging in and developing these thought processes with intention will encourage the development of positive coping strategies that will benefit people in all areas of life. The approach should begin in the home with very young children and continue throughout all levels of formal education. Education and wellbeing are intertwined, and although kindness has not been a historical focus of teaching and learning, the pandemic has shown us how important human connection, consideration, and care are to cultivating a community approach over individualism (Mehrotra, 2021). Reframing community and societal wellbeing as a top priority in education can help us learn who we are and how we fit into the world (Ulmer et al., 2020).

Positivity as a Pillar of PofK

Positivity is a branch within social psychology that explores happiness, well-being, and optimal functioning, including the types of practices and activities that those who consider themselves to be happy engage in and why those particular things influence a person's overall well-being (Brunzell et al., 2016; O'Brien & Blue, 2018). Seligman (2011) calls this concept 'flourishing' and has created the PERMA model to define well-being according to five components: positive emotions (P), engagement (E), relationships (R), meaning (M), and accomplishment (A). He considers these criteria to be some of the building blocks of wellness and found that people having one component tend to have others to a similar degree. So, how do these components of well-being inform effective pedagogy?

Combining well-being with pedagogy (the way we teach in traditional education) gives us positive pedagogy. The literature provides an extensive rationale for why positivity should be a focus in education, including that it fosters greater life satisfaction, promotes learning and creativity, decreases depression, and encourages people to keep in mind the sense of community (Chu, 2020; Kern et al., 2015; O'Brien & Blue, 2018; White & Kern, 2018). Positive learning environments cultivate constructive coping mechanisms that students and educators can use in other aspects of their lives.

Relationships are one of the five critical components of (PERMA) an acronym for positive emotion, engagement, relationships, meaning, and achievement (O'Brien & Blue, 2018). Positive psychology in education supports positive relationships between learners and teachers. These positive relationships increase learner engagement, allow learners to assign meaning more readily to their learning, and help to shape positive self-perception in learners (O'Brien & Blue, 2018). However, these authors also caution that maintaining positivity in the face of life's challenges is not an innate human characteristic; instead, people need to nourish the notion that they can overcome obstacles and achieve goals despite bumps in the road on their paths to success. The PofK provides this nourishment through caring, empathy, and compassion and leads to resilience to problems encountered (Clegg & Rowland, 2010). In turn, Brunzell et al. (2016) described a positivity spiral – the ability to increase positive emotions increases the ability to create adaptive psychological responses, which further increases positive emotions. For example, a key component of a positive learning environment that arises when using kindness in pedagogy is understanding and honouring where learners are in their lives. Honouring learners includes acknowledging their prior knowledge and experiences and encouraging them to contribute and learn in traditional and alternative ways. When teachers value these alternative and personalized approaches by students, they create a supportive atmosphere with positive emotions known to contribute to building learners' understanding of what they can achieve (Chu, 2020; O'Brien & Blue, 2018). These authors argue that education is not only a place to teach facts and thinking skills, but it is also a place that can foster learning related to broader concepts of humanism that help to create a kinder and more worthy world. This personalized and more flexible approach to teaching and learning also aligns with what Clegg and Rowland (2010) discuss as the social justice component of the PofK.

Mindfulness as a Pillar of PofK

As people face increasing demands (i.e., economic, financial, spiritual, emotional, mental, or relational), the concept of mindfulness becomes even more crucial. Education is facing increasing multi-factorial demands, particularly now under the influence of the global COVID-19 pandemic. In the past, teachers needed to confront a host of competing concerns, including falling literacy and numeracy rates, absenteeism, student engagement, student retention, large class sizes, and a burgeoning curriculum (White & Kern, 2018). When COVID-19 hit, the educators' roles (at work and home) became even more complex and demanding. For example, many educational institutions shifted to online practice. Daycares and schools closed. Teachers suddenly needed to adapt to working from home while also helping to guide their children in online education. Face-to-face teachers instantly become online educators with little to no time to transition and little to no education on nuances related to online teaching. Then, when schools reopened, teachers or other school staff became responsible for many public health and safety protocols. Teachers, who had no medical background, initiated protocols such as maintaining classroom sanitation rituals, repositioning furniture to preserve physical distancing, and cohorting learners. At the same time, educators were responsible for maintaining the pedagogical standard previously held while living in the same worldwide uncertainty as the rest of us.

Mehrotra (2021) described this as "a state of trauma, grief, and [being] overwhelmed" (p. 537). She further highlighted the paradox of views around pandemic teaching. Teachers needed to be kind, mindful, and compassionate to learners during the pandemic. They also had to uphold the neoliberal status quo idea that outcomes and productivity were the most critical factors in education and focus on the economics of education. Clegg and Rowland (2010) also identified this concept in their article. These authors lamented the politicization of education, expounding the higher value placed on measurable student achievement (related to the economy) than the acquisition of social constructs such as kindness. This paradox creates a struggle between the core values of people who enter teaching, nursing, or other caring professions and the outcomes they are required to achieve. This tension can manifest as stress.

There is no doubt that the pandemic has caused stress in the lives of many, including teachers and students. Increasing stress levels can be associated with anxiety, depression, and burnout (Crowther et al., 2021). Mindfulness has been used as a defence technique to mitigate negativity and stress (Cheli et al., 2020;

Crowther et al., 2020; Etty-Leal, 2021). The concept of mindfulness involves being fully present and self-aware, understanding psychological and physiological responses to negativity, acknowledging appropriate outcomes to situations, and processing this in a way that allows us to understand our distress and to increase our skills in relieving it (Cheli et al., 2020). In essence, mindfulness practice helps us analyze situations that may cause us to feel anxiety, panic, or depression and teaches us to acknowledge that it is okay to feel these emotions. Mindfulness also teaches positive response patterns to alleviate these feelings, feelings that may have previously debilitated us. Practicing mindfulness is a key to maintaining well-being.

Cheli et al. (2020) assert that mindfulness teaches people how to modulate their responses to situations and the behaviours of others. These authors posit that mindful-intentional strategies encourage individuals to embrace and work through uncomfortable situations rather than use their natural response of avoiding anything that makes them uneasy. So how do we begin to teach mindfulness? Mindfulness practice includes yoga, breathing exercises, guided imagery, word repetition, meditation, or positive thought exercises such as people learning to be in the moment without judgement rather than comparing themselves to others and overanalyzing situations (Fuchs et al., 2017). Over time, these authors assert that the ability to focus heightens with mindfulness practice and leads to increased recognition of one's ways of self-processing, including the occurrence of misrepresented or exaggerated negative emotions.

Intentionally integrating mindfulness-based interventions into pedagogy early and throughout a person's life builds on resilience and relational capacities (Brunzell et al., 2016). Brunzell et al. (2016) assert that improved magnitude in these areas allows for increased psychological regulatory capacity and decreases stress resulting in benefits across the human experience. Learning to mitigate negative feelings and respond in a positive, constructive manner is a skill that will serve people well in all areas of their lives by decreasing reactionary, unnecessary responses. Mindful practices fall easily into the PofK because foundational human values are inherent in both. That is, when we learn to understand and value human experiences, thoughts, and processes through employing kindness, care, compassion, and empathy, we discover our capacities to grow and learn. Being kind and mindful can be applied at the individual, community, or global level to help us be understanding of ourselves and others.

Gratitude as a Pillar of PofK

Gratitude is a positive emotion experienced when one unexpectedly receives something perceived as having value (Chu, 2020; Fournier & Sheehan, 2015). The integration of gratitude exercises is a positive pedagogical strategy that helps to foster growth mindsets and resilience amongst learners while decreasing symptoms of stress, depression, and anxiety (Chu, 2020). Easily implemented activities associated with gratitude include simple ideas such as inviting learners to state what they are thankful for or asking them to write a letter to someone who has positively impacted their life.

This gratitude process aligns well with the PofK. Educators following a teaching philosophy based on the PofK acknowledge and respect learners' past experiences, their decisions about the learning process, and how they interpret and react to the world around them. The humanistic approach of treating people as a compilation of all their experiences, rather than only those experiences they choose to present, offers insight into potential and growth. Humanistic educators teach students that there is value in everything they do if they can only find the silver lining.

Employing gratitude exercises in post-secondary education encourages learners to think with a more collective/community approach and increases empathy in their interactions with others (Chu, 2020). Educators that integrate positivity, mindfulness, and gratitude into pedagogy help students build their psychological toolbox to meet the challenges they face in schools and other aspects of their lives. Intentionally teaching people to focus on the positive cultivates that natural positivity spiral described earlier. Additionally, Chu (2020) and Fournier and Sheehan (2015) report that gratitude activities encourage people to think beyond themselves. When we stimulate this kind of decentralization, we can increase empathy and even incite positive movements focused on helping others.

Integrating Positivity, Mindfulness, and Gratitude into the Pedagogy of Kindness

Kindness is not a new tenet of effective teaching practice. Kindness is a quality that is recognized but not emphasized in the literature despite learners rating it highly on their list of qualities that make a "good" teacher (Clegg & Rowland, 2010). Clegg and Rowland (2010) highlight the virtues of teachers being kind and discuss the contrarian opinion exposed by many in higher education that kind teachers are "soft" and use kindness to avoid engaging learners or overlook errors. The truth is an educator can be kind and value academic achievement – this is not an either/or concept.

The crisis of the COVID-19 pandemic has made us acutely aware of the value of kindness in all aspects of life (including education). The shared human experience of a global pandemic has alerted us that we cannot simply move along demanding the same outcomes and productivity of educators and learners (well, really, of anyone) without considering the additional stresses from COVID and the unknowns it creates. At the very least, we need to acknowledge the adjustments we have had to make to many aspects of our lives and that when others are kind (and we are kind to others and ourselves), we are more successful in adapting to our new realities.

While there is limited guidance on how to increase well-being in schools, many scholars have supported using kindness in pedagogy. Kern et al. (2015) recommended, years before this pandemic, that it was time to consider and value holistic human experience. Further, these authors recommended that schools, where many children and youth spend much of their time, are prime locations to cultivate self-worth. Educators using kindness, care, empathy and compassion (as well as positivity, mindfulness, and gratitude) in pedagogy encourage students to be self-aware and self-confident and value themselves and others.

Teachers who role-model a PofK are open, accessible, and welcoming when interacting with learners. These teachers surrender the idea that learners are the "enemy" from whom they expect the worst (Denial, 2019). Denial (2019) also recommends that if a teacher's first instinct is not to respond to a situation with compassion, they should step back and reflect on why they are reacting that way. Attempting to meet students where they are at in their educational journeys while actively promoting positivity, mindfulness, and gratitude can lead to deeper and more meaningful learning and more effective educator/learner relationships.

Teachers have the power to ignite the positivity spiral repeatedly, successfully fueling increased educator and learner satisfaction.

As Santovec (2021) writes, "The pedagogy of kindness is centered around three principles: justice, believing people, and believing in people" (p. 11). Santovec (2021) recommends implementing these practices into pedagogy by reading about kindness, empathy, caring, compassion, positivity, mindfulness and gratitude, and thinking about what you know versus what you want to know. This author further suggests thinking about if the learning environment fosters opportunities for student engagement and discussion and trying to enact these principles in interactions with individuals, groups, and communities. The goal is always to try to bring positivity and community outcomes to the fore for all topics. White and Kern (2018) summarize this intention: "if we are to be fully human, we must be active citizens helping to create a flourishing state" (p. 3).

Conclusion

The foundation of the PofK is the acknowledgement of the human experience. If we can appreciate the uniqueness of individual experiences and acknowledge that these experiences enable us all to learn, we can cultivate a community that supports one another. The simple acts of being kind, compassionate, caring, and empathetic open us up to new levels of understanding, which promote a more intense ability to connect with others. The result of these series of events is to foster resilience and confidence in individuals who have a strong sense of community. When you consistently remind people of what they can do instead of what they cannot do, you create a culture of possibility. A culture of possibility is the fuel of unlimited potential. What would it mean to the teaching and learning praxis if we always began from this incredible consideration? The sky's the limit.

References

Brunzell, T., Stokes, H., & Waters, L. (2016). Trauma-informed positive
    education: Using positive psychology to strengthen vulnerable students.
    Contemporary School Psychology, 20, 63-83.
    https://doi.org/10.1007/s40688-015-0070-x

Cheli, S., de Bartolo, P., & Agostini, A.A. (2020). Integrating mindfulness into
    nursing education: A pilot nonrandomized controlled trial. *International
    Journal of Stress Management, 27*(1), 93-100.
    https://doi.org/10.1037/str0000126

Chu, T.L. (2020). Applying positive psychology to foster student engagement and
    classroom community amid the COVID-19 pandemic and beyond.
    Scholarship of Teaching and Learning in Psychology. Advance online
    publication. https://doi.org/10.1037/stl0000238

Clegg, S., & Rowland, S. (2010). Kindness in pedagogical practice and academic
    life. *British Journal of Sociology of Education, 31*(6), 719-735.
    https://doi.org/10.1080/01425692.2010.515102

Crowther, L.L.., Robertson, N., & Anderson, E.S. (2020). Mindfulness for
    undergraduate health and social care professional students: Findings from
    a qualitative scoping review using the 3P model. *Medical Education in
    Review, 54*, 796-810. https://doi.org/10.1111/medu.14150

Denial, C. (2019). *A pedagogy of kindness*. https://hybridpedagogy.org/pedagogy-
    of-kindness

Etty-Leal, J. (2021). Making mindfulness matter to children: Holistic, heartful,
    and creative mindful education. *The Humanistic Psychologist, 40*(1), 190-
    201. http://doi.org/10.1037/hum0000184

Fournier, A., & Sheehan, C. (2015). Growing gratitude in undergraduate nursing
    students: Applying findings from social and psychological domains to
    nursing education. *Nurse Education Today, 35*, 1139-1141.
    http://doi.org/10.1016/j.nedt.2015.08.010

Fuchs, W. W., Mundschenk, N. J., & Groark, B. (2017). A promising practice:
    School-based mindfulness-based stress reduction strategies for children
    with disabilities. *Journal of International Special Needs Education, 20*(2),
    56-66. https://doi.org/10.9782/2159-4341-20.2.56

Mehrotra, G.R. (2021). Centering a pedagogy of care in the pandemic. *Qualitative Social Work, 20*(1-2), 537-543. Http://doi.org/10.1177//1473325020981079

Kern, M.L., Waters, L.E., Adler, A., & White, M.A. (2015). A multidimensional approach to measuring well-being in students: Application of the PERMA framework. *The Journal of Positive Psychology, 10*(3), 262-271. http://doi.org/10.1080/17439760.2014.936962

O'Brien, M., & Blue, L. (2018). Towards a positive pedagogy: Designing pedagogical practices that facilitate positivity within the classroom. *Educational Action Research, 26*(3), 365-384. https://doi.org/10.1080/09650792.2017.1339620

Santovec, M.L. (2021). Developing and practicing a pedagogy of kindness. *Women in Higher Education, 30*(7), 11-15. https://doi.org/10.1002/whe.21013

Seligman, F. (2011). *Flourish.* Simon & Schuster.

Ulmer, J.B., Kuby, C.R., & Christ, R.C. (2020) What do pedagogies produce? Thinking/teaching qualitative inquiry. *Qualitative Inquiry, 26*(1), 3-12. http://doi.org/10.1177//1077800419869961

Chapter Six:

The Relevance of a Pedagogy of Kindness as Educators Shifted to Online Teaching During the Coronavirus Pandemic

By Elizabeth Gorny-Wegrzyn and Beth Perry

Chapter Six presents a summary and analysis of the scholarly and grey literature on COVID-19 and how this novel coronavirus has affected higher education and changed current teaching practice. Many students were required to study online due to the measures used to stop the spread of COVID-19. While the pandemic precipitated a rapid move from face-to-face to online teaching and learning, this change may likely be permanent for some. Educators who needed to become skilled at online teaching almost overnight sought pedagogical approaches to help their teaching be effective in this new medium. PofK was one approach some teachers moving to online found valuable.

This chapter addresses the questions: how did the coronavirus pandemic change current teaching practice in higher education, and what steps did educators take to continue to deliver quality education through an online approach? From the perspective of teachers, students, and researchers: in what ways is online education as effective as face-to-face teaching, and by what means can electronically mediated instruction engage students, provide stimulating learning environments, and facilitate the achievement of learning outcomes? Finally, what are some teaching strategies (using the underpinnings of a PofK) that can help increase the efficacy of online instruction?

The literature revealed that COVID-19 necessitated many educators to employ a completely online approach to course delivery. Instructors had to adapt their teaching strategies and styles and reorganize their classes to be effective online. Specifically, educators had to wholly embrace a learner-centred teaching approach and be especially mindful of students' unique learning needs. Using pedagogies such as the PofK with teaching approaches like arts-based instruction engages students fully, helps create stimulating learning environments, and positively impacts learning outcomes in online learning environments. The use of kindness, care, empathy, and compassion facilitates online instruction that is more open and inviting for students, making it engaging and effective.

Chapter Objectives

After completing chapter six the reader will be able to

- Describe how COVID-19 changed current teaching practice in higher education
- Explain how educators can deliver quality education through an online mode using a PofK
- Name several effective online teaching strategies and philosophies that use kindness, care, empathy, and compassion in their teaching approach

Introduction

"When we least expect it, life sets us a challenge to test our courage and willingness to change; at such a moment, there is no point in pretending that nothing has happened or in saying that we are not yet ready. The challenge will not wait. Life does not look back."– Paulo Coelho (Scott, 2019).

The severe acute respiratory syndrome coronavirus 2 (SARS-CoV-2), also known as (COVID-19), has irrevocably changed the world. There are presently over 85 million confirmed COVID-19 cases and 1.8 million deaths worldwide, and these numbers increase daily (World Health Organization [WHO], 2020). Every aspect of daily human life has been affected by this deadly disease. In response, we have had no choice but to radically change how we undertake activities such as work, travel, health care, education, socialization, etc. (Dans, 2020). The global population had to adopt new ways of existing and interacting in their social and physical environments. Through many challenges and uncertainties of the past year, the public showed that they could survive and thrive due to resiliency, adaptability, and coming together as an international community to combat this disease. WHO (2020) writes that global collaboration is helping in the fight against this novel coronavirus and its dire effects on the world, "leading health experts from around the world have been meeting at the World Health Organization's Geneva headquarters to assess the current level of knowledge about the new COVID-19 disease, identify gaps and work together to accelerate and fund priority research needed to help stop this outbreak and prepare for any future outbreaks." (Para. 1). Also, individual communities, institutions, and organizations have put preventative measures into place (social distancing, frequent hand washing, and wearing masks when out in public) to help stop the spread of COVID-19 (WHO, 2020).

Precautionary measures instituted to control the coronavirus have touched every part of our lives, including education. Educators, academic administrators and staff, researchers, and students have had to accept and adapt to social distancing as the new norm. Due to the pandemic and the preventative interventions instituted, most colleges and universities have changed their primary mode of teaching delivery from face-to-face and blended models to a completely online approach (Altbach & De Wit, 2020; Bates, 2020; Houlden & Veletsianos, 2020; Hughes, 2020; Rapanta, Botturi, Goodyear, et al., 2020). To meet the challenge of the transition from in-class teaching to an online milieu, educators had to prepare themselves to deliver effective and quality online education.

The purpose of this chapter was to review and analyze the literature on the effects the coronavirus has had on the delivery of higher education, specifically the transition from teaching students face-to-face to providing education in a completely online mode. The specific focus of the chapter is the relevance of a PofK with this shift to teaching online. The questions of interest that guided this review included: how did this pandemic change current teaching practice in higher education, and what measures did educators take to continue to deliver quality education using an online method? From the perspectives of researchers, teachers, and students: in what ways is online education as effective as face-to-face teaching, and by what means can online courses engage students, provide stimulating learning environments, and facilitate the achievement of learning outcomes? Finally, what teaching strategies can help improve online learners' academic success, and can these strategies increase online education's effectiveness?

While it is impossible to address all these questions in totality in this chapter, these questions are all related to the common overarching question of the impact of COVID 19 on higher education. This chapter provides readers with an overview of the current literature that may be foundational for more extensive analyses and investigations.

Changes in Teaching Practice in Higher Education due to Pandemic: Analysis of the Literature

The worldwide coronavirus pandemic required educators and university administrators to urgently change their teaching delivery methods due to the precautions established to decrease the spread of COVID-19. As social distancing became a necessity, the face-to-face teaching method was changed (almost immediately) to a completely online instruction mode (Altbach & De Wit, 2020; Houlden & Veletsianos, 2020; Rapanta et al., 2020). Altbach and De Wit (2020) write that with over 20,000 universities and 200 million students worldwide, we cannot generalize how these safety measures affected all universities or student populations. Some universities may thrive and become stronger through this pandemic, while others (poorly funded or in lower-income countries) may suffer and fail (Altbach & De Wit, 2020). However, we can determine that the COVID-19 pandemic globally changed the predominant instructional delivery method in higher education. Importantly, changing the means of teaching delivery is not a straightforward matter and requires careful planning. As well, specialized teaching skills and knowledge are needed to provide quality online education. In brief, teaching online is not the same as teaching face-to-face.

Online Teaching Methods and Technologies

To deliver quality online education, instructors must first consider the unique qualities and needs of learners who study at a distance and then structure online courses that can maintain interest and motivation and enable students' continued participation (Ching et al., 2018). The "instructional design" (the planning, organization, and structuring of a course) is of vital importance to effective online teaching and considering the individualities of a diverse student population is critical when planning this design (Ching et al., 2018).

Bates (2020) advises using an institutional learning management system (LMS) as it provides structure for a course and supplies a schedule for lectures and due dates for class assignments. Bates (2019) describes a LMS layout, "these provide a weekly structure for lessons, organize content in the form of text or online readings, provide a forum for discussion on course topics, provide regular online activities and assignments, and could include links to short videos" (chapter 4.2.2). Bates (2019, 2020) encourages educators to work collaboratively with instructional designers as they are knowledgeable regarding technology and effective course construction while educators can contribute course content, assessment strategies, and learning activities.

Bates (2019) cautions that although the main structure of the LMS is like an in-class arrangement, there are differences between in-class (face-to-face) and electronic courses, and effective educators tailor online syllabi to meet the learning goals of students studying at a distance. Online course content is mostly text-based and accessed at the learner's convenience at any time, and course discussions are online and usually asynchronous (Bates, 2019, 2020). These characteristics make online classes more flexible and autonomous for learners, but instructors must adapt their teaching strategies to stimulate student engagement, motivation, and participation (Bates, 2019, 2020; Kebritchi et al., 2017).

Bates (2019, 2020) suggests approaches such as employing lecture capture (to record and stream lectures instead of streaming live), ZOOM videos for more personalized student contact, avoiding overly long presentations, and even encouraging students to create course content themselves. Bates recommends that online teaching design be organized, structured, and personalized and that educators must be empathetic to learners who come from various backgrounds and have different needs. Houlden and Veletsianos (2020) agree that to provide effective, engaging, and enriching learning experiences, online educators should work as partners with instructional designers who can help them teach skillfully with technology while also being attentive to individual student priorities.

Therefore, it is critically important for educators who are changing from face-to-face to online instruction due to COVID-19 (or for any other reason) to embrace a wholly learner-centered approach to teaching. Learners suddenly moved to online courses often come from diverse backgrounds, and educators need to be especially mindful of students' unique learning needs. The diversity of ability or interest in learning online, and individuality of learning goals and requirements, is accentuated as students accustomed to face-to-face learning are suddenly shifted to online instruction (Bates, 2019, 2020; Kebritchi et al., 2017).

Fawns (2019) warns that some LMSs and instructional designs may have pedagogies embedded in them by the developers that support educational hierarchies and power inequalities in higher education and that may not be congruent with an instructor's educational philosophy. Fawns (2019) argues that teaching practices are often situational and relative to the immediate circumstances, and therefore effective instructors change their teaching strategies as situations with learners change. Fawns (2019) writes about teaching practices, stating, "they are structured, to some extent, by institutional expectations and policies, but they are also situated and contextual, emerging out of a complex tapestry of conditions and parameters that cannot be predetermined" (para. 16). In other words, Fawns (2019) suggests that teaching practice and learning are contextualized and should consider the actions and behaviours of teachers and students and their interactions with each other. These behaviours and interplays between students and teachers and among students can change in different circumstances. Fawns (2019) does not support instructional designs based only on student tasks and thinks courses should include social interactions supported by participative learning environments. Also, these models should invite collaboration among educators and learners so that students can help construct teaching and learning practice as partners with instructors (Fawns, 2019). Fawns (2019) concludes that extensive reliance on very structured LMSs and pre-established course content detracts from achieving learning goals. Instructors who follow a teaching philosophy based on a PofK are empathetic towards students and collaborate as equal partners in class decisions, making learning environments more favourable for academic success.

Ching et al. (2018) note that many teachers do not follow any instructional design model and instead configure their online courses informally because some educators may not know an instructional model exists, while others feel that these models restrict the creativity and flexibility of their classes. Ching et al. (2018) describe how some instructors informally configure a syllabus for online use. The authors write that educators usually use an existing outline with course objectives, collect online resources, structure and chuck content, consider the class size and the knowledge level of students, and then distribute assignments and course activities (Ching et al., 2018).

Whether teachers use an instructional model or not, most educators prefer to adapt the course design as the class proceeds often based on feedback from students (Ching et al., 2018). Ching et al. suggest that instructional designers must try to understand how teachers structure informal course designs. The developers should use teachers' input when designing an instructional model, as educators know what is effective in motivating students and in producing stimulating learning environments (Ching et al., 2018). These co-created instructional models could be used by educators more willingly and successfully.

Educators as Designers

Not only is it essential for developers to construct instructional designs based on educators' input regarding effective teaching, but it is also paramount to ensure educators are knowledgeable about learning design fundamentals. McKenney et al. (2015) encourage further research on developing professional programs to assist teachers in learning design methods. Increasingly educators are already often doing more than just planning class lessons; they also "design new learning activities and create their own (technology-enhanced) learning materials" (McKenney et al., 2015, p. 2). The need for instituting professional design programs, educating teachers on instructional design fundamentals (or giving them access to designer team members), has become even more crucial during the COVID-19 pandemic as education moved online. If educators do not have some knowledge and skills related to effective online course design (and in many cases, teachers do not have access to instructional designers) the quality of instruction will likely be hampered.

McKenney et al. (2015) write about the three components of instructional design models: technical, phenomenological, and realist. The technical element includes design thinking and problem solving and emphasizes design models and outlines (McKenney et al., 2015). The technical component of design provides guidelines, analysis, testing, and planning tools. Historically, this aspect did not consider the human factor, but recently the design process has included contextual matters, human values, empathy, and collaboration (McKenney et al., 2015). The phenomenological aspect of design includes designers' reflections and places value on teachers' intuition and experience (McKenney et al., 2015). The realist portion of the design process deals with practical concerns: the level of design expertise, the knowledge of technology, and the capacity to blend technological and pedagogical knowledge to teach effectively using technology (McKenney et al., 2015). Teachers as designers need to integrate their understanding of course content, pedagogy, and technology for effective online teaching practice, more so now due to the pandemic. Having a carefully planned design for teaching practice (incorporating the technical, phenomenological, and realist elements) can help educators deliver quality education, furnish stimulating learning environments, and facilitate positive learning outcomes in an online milieu.

Online Teaching Strategies

Effective teaching strategies used by instructors (especially outstanding educators) facilitate expanding learners' ways of knowing and encourages them to think independently. Hughes (2020) writes that "university is embedded in the bedrock of intellectual production, intellectual freedom and even resistance to dictatorial thought" (para. 16). The social meetings, organizations, and clubs university students participate in allow for an open exchange of thought, stimulate social activism, and lead to social change (Hughes, 2020). The COVID-19 pandemic has changed learners' social interactions and limited in-person sharing of ideas. Educators working in online settings are responsible for providing learning environments that still engage students, support an exchange of thoughts regarding social injustice, and heighten social awareness. Being successful in providing a stimulating learning environment that captures students' interest also motivates learners to participate more fully in their studies and positively impacts learning outcomes (Serbati et al., 2020). Yet, what teaching philosophies and strategies are productive, especially in a completely online learning environment?

The literature shows that educators who embrace teaching philosophies based on pedagogies like the PofK that encourage a free exchange of ideas, independent thought, and teacher-student collaboration engage students in academic and social activities and positively impact learning environments, improve learning outcomes, and enhance social consciousness (Breuing, 2011; hooks, 2003; Serbati et al., 2020). Educators who espouse pedagogies like the pedagogy of hope or the PofK follow a teaching philosophy where instructors and learners work together as equal partners in the teaching and learning process, valuing, and respecting each other (hooks, 2003; Serbati et al., 2020). In sum, teaching philosophies that include kindness, care, empathy, and compassion empower students, make them feel worthy as humans, guide them in seeing the worth in others, and heighten their awareness of social inequities. Such approaches seem especially apt as teaching moves online, and instructors and learners are separated by distance.

The literature also shows that educators who use innovative techniques during their online classes, such as visual aids, creative instructional strategies, or humour, can capture students' interest and keep them engaged (Serbati et al., 2020). These teaching approaches are just as beneficial online as they are in face-to-face instruction as they are learner-centred and rely on collaboration and feedback from students (Kebritchi et al., 2017; Rapanta et al., 2020). Instructors who use these teaching techniques are organized, enthusiastic, and can communicate with clarity, and they are also empathetic and can understand the unique needs of diverse student populations (Hativa et al., 2001; Serbati et al., 2020). Educators who follow a teaching philosophy based on a PofK understand and empathize with students and form educator-learner relationships (based on mutual trust and respect) that promote enriching learning environments and enhance the achievement of learning outcomes (Hativa et al., 2001; Serbati et al., 2020).

Rapanta et al. (2020) highlight, in their interviews with highly successful educators, that online education must be learner-centred, taking into consideration thoughts and feedback from students. Lourdes Guàrdia asserts in his reflection, in the Rapanta et al. study, that face-to-face instruction is mainly teacher-centred and relies on conventional lecture-style delivery, where successful online teaching is collaborative and involves meaningful class activities (2020). Guàrdia, in the article by Rapanta et al. (2020), writes, "a learner-centred approach is a key issue in online learning models, but it does not eliminate the teacher. A learner-centred environment facilitates a more collaborative way for students to learn, and the teacher acts as a facilitator, providing feedback and answering questions when needed. The teacher should design meaningful learning activities, based on authentic learning, contextualizing learning situations as much as possible" (E3). Therefore, to be successful in online instruction, educators must adopt strategies that feature meaningful learning activities, are enjoyable, stimulate curiosity, and increase motivation and participation in the learning process. These strategies align perfectly with a PofK.

Arts-Based Pedagogy

Contact North (2020) writes that 1.5 billion students worldwide took part in some remote learning during the peak of the first wave of the pandemic. At that time, faculty in universities looked for teaching strategies that engaged online students in academic activities, made higher education more accessible and flexible, increased the sharing of power between teacher and learner, and enhanced the use of innovative technology (Contact North, 2020).

Arts-based pedagogy (ABP) is a teaching practice that can stimulate learners' curiosity, motivation, and participation in online class activities (Perry & Edwards, 2019). ABP integrates an art form with course subject matter to positively influence student learning (Rieger et al., 2016). Boston University. (n. d.) defines arts-based learning as "the purposeful use of artistic skills, processes, and experiences as educational tools to foster learning in non-artistic disciplines and domains" (para. 1). Arts-based instruction enhances learners' creativity and problem-solving skills and helps students achieve solutions in inventive and original ways (Carleton University, 2020).

Rieger et al. (2020), in their constructivist grounded theory study of nursing students and nursing instructors, examined how educators who employed an ABP nurtured meaningful learning for students. The authors found that through arts-based instruction, learners used both divergent and convergent thinking processes. Students also engaged in self-reflection and self-evaluation of their work, and they received (and found) informal peer evaluation to be beneficial (Rieger et al., 2020). Exchanges with instructors during the ABP process were supportive and facilitated students finding a deeper meaning to their learning. As well, an earlier study done by Rieger et al. (2016) concluded that "ABP appears to facilitate learning in the cognitive and affective domains and may be especially useful in addressing the affective domain" (para. results). These studies showed that arts-based teaching fostered creative thinking in learners and resulted in nursing students developing original thoughts and finding solutions to eventually apply in practice (Rieger et al., 2020).

In the same sense, Perry and Edwards (2019), in their follow-up study on innovative arts-based learning approaches adapted for mobile learning, reaffirmed their previous research findings that arts-based instructional strategies facilitate academic accomplishment. Arts-based instruction is a collaborative learning process that can help students feel they are part of a community and decrease feelings of isolation that distance learners often experience (Perry & Edwards, 2019). The authors state, "interaction, social presence, and the sense of community were enhanced when arts-based approaches were used, in part because they encouraged creativity, helped to build rapport among participants, personalized interactions, cultivated trust, and promoted learner control" (Perry & Edwards, 2019, para. 1). During COVID-19, students who suddenly find themselves learning alone at home with their laptops instead of in classrooms may be particularly craving the social interactions and sense of community that ABP provides.

Perry and Edwards (2019) used effective arts-based instructional techniques for computer-assisted education and adapted them for mobile devices. Arts-based techniques like poetweet, photo pairing, reflective mosaic, and six-word story help students achieve affective domain learning outcomes (Perry & Edwards, 2019). These techniques encourage learners to reflect on course material in a deeper and more meaningful way; explore human feelings, attitudes, biases, and values; openly discuss thought-provoking subjects; and be innovative when sharing their thoughts with classmates and teachers (Perry & Edwards, 2019). In brief, arts-based instruction engages students, facilities academic achievement, promotes creative thinking, encourages complex problem solving, advances communication skills, and enhances academic competencies.

Finally, ABP encourages holistic learning by propelling students to draw on their own experiences when contributing to discussions of thought-evoking topics (Van Katwyk et al., 2019). Arts-based teaching and learning foster inquiry and discourse on power and privilege, thereby facilitating a deeper understanding of social inequities, and enhancing awareness of social injustices (Van Katwyk et al., 2019). Seifter (2016) concluded that arts-based learning enhances student behaviours such as sharing, active and empathic listening, and feelings of mutual respect and trust. These behaviours encourage students from diverse backgrounds to openly share their thoughts regarding different life experiences heightening their awareness of social justice (Seifter. 2016; Van Katwyk et al., 2019). Briefly, ABP furnishes stimulating learning environments that engage students and increases participation in class activities, including meaningful discussions, thereby facilitating the achievement of learning outcomes and enhancing social consciousness. During COVID lockdowns educators forced to move from a face-to-face learning environment (where achievement of socioemotional learning outcomes often occurs quite naturally through informal conversations and social interactions) to teaching online need to find new strategies to achieve these affective domain learning goals. The earlier research on APB described above may provide some ideas for educators who are looking for instructional approaches that align with a PofK.

Results and Discussion

In reviewing the literature, three themes became evident. First, the global delivery of education in universities moved almost entirely from a face-to-face teaching method to a completely online mode because of the precautions instituted to decrease the spread of the novel coronavirus, COVID-19. Educators had to adapt their teaching practice quickly, moving from a face-to-face to an online milieu. This adjustment to electronic instruction is not a simple transition and requires specialized teaching abilities, knowledge, and careful preparation on the part of teachers. Educators must gain these new online teaching skills to continue delivering quality education as likely some instruction will remain online post-pandemic.

Second, educators who made the transition from face-to-face to online teaching effectively adopted a wholly student-centred and collaborative teaching approach focused on addressing the unique needs of students learning at a distance (Bates, 2020; Rapanta et al., 2020). Instructional designs, both formal and informal, and LMSs were beneficial in planning and structuring online classes and creating stimulating, enriching, and motivating learning environments that engaged students and increased their participation in class activities (Bates, 2020; Houlden & Veletsianos, 2020). As well, adopting teaching philosophies and strategies, like a PofK, and using methods such as arts-based instruction, were valuable in engaging students, enhancing the learning experience, facilitating the achievement of learning outcomes, encouraging discourse on social justice, and heightening social awareness (Rieger et al., 2020; Perry & Edwards, 2019; Van Katwyk et al., 2019).

Finally, from the perspective of teachers, students, and researchers, online education that uses teaching strategies and technologies that are stimulating, engaging, and motivating can be just as effective as face-to-face teaching (Bates, 2020; Perry & Edwards, 2019; Rapanta et al., 2020). With well-developed skills, new knowledge, and careful planning, teachers successfully transitioned from in-class instruction to teaching online. Educators who become skillful and knowledgeable about teaching in an online milieu can be just as successful in delivering quality education in this environment as they were in physical classrooms (Houlden & Veletsianos, 2020; Rapanta et al., 2020). Students taking online courses from instructors who use constructive and valuable teaching strategies are just as motivated in their studies and achieve as much academically and socially as students in face-to-face settings (Serbati et al., 2020).

Online instruction uses a constructivism philosophy where learning is an active process (Rieger et al., 2020). As noted in Chapter One, constructivism is a learning theory based on cognitive psychology, where students acquire knowledge through the interactions of personal experiences, ideas, and the learning environment (Bates, 2019; Rieger et al., 2020). Gogus (2012) writes that students in a constructivist learning environment "generate knowledge and meaning from their experiences, mental structures, and beliefs that are used to interpret objects and events. Constructivism focuses on the importance of the individual knowledge, beliefs, and skills through the experience of learning" (para. definition). In other words, the constructivism theory infers that students actively learn when they interpret information in the context of their own experiences and understand this new information by combining it with their prior knowledge (Bates, 2019; Gogus, 2012). Online instruction using student-centred and constructivist learning philosophies like a PofK and arts-based instruction can deliver effective and quality education.

In sum, the COVID-19 pandemic taught us that online education can be, and is, as beneficial as in-class instruction if instructors are well-prepared and teaching and learning approaches are adapted to address learners' needs and focus on the unique challenges of remote learning.

Conclusion

Chapter Six examined the impact of the move to online teaching and learning precipitated by COVID-19. The elements included in the analysis of the literature were how educators accomplished the transition from in-class teaching to online instruction while maintaining the quality of education. The literature indicated that educators had to take several actions to make this process successful. When transitioning to an online teaching milieu: educators considered the distinctive needs of online learners, educational approaches changed from teacher-centred to wholly student-centred, and learners, peers, and instructors shared the learning process as partners (Bates, 2020; Rapanta et al., 2020). Educators had to plan and structure courses suitable for online instruction, and in doing so, teachers had to create classes that motivated and engaged students and facilitated class participation (Bates, 2019, 2020; Ching et al., 2018; Houlden & Veletsianos, 2020). Planning productive online courses requires a certain amount of expertise and understanding of instructional design, and many teachers need further education on this process. Most teachers thrust into being online educators due to COVID-19 did not have the expertise they needed to be immediately comfortable within this learning environment (Bates, 2019, 2020; Ching et al., 2018; Houlden & Veletsianos, 2020). Last, the literature revealed that using pedagogies like the PofK, and teaching strategies such as ABP, can make online teaching and learning an enriching experience and have the potential to improve learning outcomes and enhance social awareness (Rieger et al., 2016, 2020; Perry & Edwards, 2019; Seifter. 2016; Van Katwyk et al., 2019).

COVID-19 has had a profound impact on the way education is delivered. It has likely changed the mode of delivery permanently as many teachers and students now prefer the online milieu (Altbach & De Wit, 2020). Preliminary research shows that teachers skilled in face-to-face instruction need to develop new skills and knowledge to ensure their online teaching is equally skillful. As many educators are now moving online, we need more research to provide instructors with strategies in creating successful online courses, either independently or with the support of learning designers. Educators new to teaching online require instruction in planning, structuring, and delivering courses in this mode. Due to COVID-19, educators who were skilled at teaching face-to-face had to move to online instruction as students were required to move to distance education. Without adequate preparation, educators facing this transition were disadvantaged. Studies on how to instruct educators on effective online teaching are necessary to prepare them. Also, additional research exploring which teaching strategies can best foster meaningful online learning is needed.

As noted above, likely academic institutions will continue to offer online or hybrid models of teaching post-pandemic. Contact North (2020) writes that this abrupt transition into online instruction has colleges and universities investigating the best instructional online methods for "beyond the pandemic" (para. 6). The PofK and ABP are effective in online education, but researching these and other, successful approaches related to exemplary online teaching and learning is a priority.

References

Altbach, P. G., & De Wit, H. (2020). Postpandemic outlook for higher education is bleakest for the poorest. *International Higher Education, 102*, 3–5. https://www.internationalhighereducation.net/api-v1/article/!/action/getPdfOfArticle/articleID/2904/productID/29/filename/article-id-2904.pdf

Bates, A. W. (2019). *Teaching in a digital age.* 2nd Edition. Vancouver: Tony Bates Associates. https://teachonline.ca/teaching-in-a-digital-age/teaching-in-a-digital-age-second-edition

Bates, A. W. (2020). Advice to those about to teach online because of the corona-virus. *Online Learning and Distant Education Resources.* https://www.tonybates.ca/2020/03/09/advice-to-those-about-to-teach-online-because-of-the-corona-virus/.

Boston University. (n. d.). Arts-based learning. *Center for Teaching and Learning.* https://www.bu.edu/ctl/guides/arts-based-learning/

Breuing, M. (2011). Problematizing critical pedagogy. *International Journal of Critical Pedagogy, 3*(3), 1-23. https://www.marybreunig.com/assets/files/Problematizing%20Critical%20Pedagogy.pdf

Carleton University. (2020). Arts-based learning. *Experiential Education.* https://carleton.ca/experientialeducation/in-class-experiential-education/arts-based-learning/

Ching, Y.-H., Hsu, Y.-C., & Baldwin, S. (2018). Becoming an online teacher: an analysis of prospective online instructors' reflections. *Journal of Interactive Learning Research, 29*(2), 145–168. https://doi.org/10.24059/olj.v22i2.1212.

Contact North. (August 04, 2020). A new pedagogy is emerging... and online learning is a key contributing factor. *Teachonline.ca* https://teachonline.ca/tools-trends/how-teach-online-student-success/new-pedagogy-emerging-and-online-learning-key-contributing-factor

Dans, E. (2020, July 26). The pandemic really has changed the world forever. *Forbes.* https://www.forbes.com/sites/enriquedans/2020/07/26/the-pandemic-really-has-changed-the-worldforever/?sh=586962a736a6

Fawns, T. (2019). Postdigital education in design and practice. *Postdigital Science and Education, 1*(1), 132–145. https://doi.org/10.1007/s42438-018-0021-8.

Gogus A. (2012) Constructivist Learning. In: Seel N.M. (eds) *Encyclopedia of the Sciences of Learning*. Springer, Boston, MA. https://doi.org/10.1007/978-1-4419-1428-6_142

Hativa, N., Barak, R., & Simhi, E. (2001). Exemplary university teachers: Knowledge and beliefs regarding effective teaching dimensions and strategies. *The Journal of Higher Education, 72*(6), 699-729. http://www.jstor.org/stable/2672900

hooks, b. (2003). *Teaching Community: A Pedagogy of Hope*. New York: Routledge

Houlden, S., & Veletsianos, G. (2020). Coronavirus pushes universities to switch to online classes – but are they ready? *The Conversation.* https://theconversation.com/coronaviruspushes-universities-to-switch-to-online-classes-but-arethey-ready-132728.

Hughes, C. (2020). COVID-19, higher education and the impact on society: what we know so far and what could happen. *World Economic Forum.* https://www.weforum.org/agenda/2020/11/covid-19-higher-education-and-the-impact-on-society-what-we-know-so-far-and-what-could-happen/

Kebritchi, M., Lipschuetz, A., & Santiague, L. (2017). Issues and challenges for teaching successful online courses in higher education: A literature review. *Journal of Educational Technology Systems, 46.* 4-29. 10.1177/0047239516661713. https://www.researchgate.net/publication/319013030_Issues_and_Challenges_for_Teaching_Successful_Online_Courses_in_Higher_Education_A_Literature_Review

McKenney, S., Kali, Y., Markauskaite, L., & Voogt, J. (2015). Teacher design knowledge for technology enhanced learning: an ecological framework for investigating assets and needs. *Instructional Science, 43*(2), 181-202. https://doi.org/10.1007/s11251-014-9337-2.

Perry, B & Edwards, M. (2019). Innovative arts-based learning approaches adapted for mobile learning. *Open Praxis, 11*(3). https://doi.org/10.5944/openpraxis.11.3.967

Pili, O. (2014). LMS vs. SNS: Can social networking sites act as a learning management system? *American International Journal of Contemporary Research,* 4(5), 1-8. http://www.aijcrnet.com/journals/Vol_4_No_5_May_2014/9.pdf

Rapanta, C., Botturi, L., Goodyear, P. et al. (2020). Online university teaching during and after the Covid-19 crisis: Refocusing teacher presence and learning activity. *Postdigit Sci Educ,* 2, 923–945 https://doi.org/10.1007/s42438-020-00155-y

Rieger, K. L., Chernomas, W. M., McMillan, D. E., & Morin, F. L. (2020). Navigating creativity within arts-based pedagogy: Implications of a constructivist grounded theory study. *Nurse Education Today, 91.* https://doi.org/10.1016/j.nedt.2020.104465

Rieger, K. L., Chernomas, W. M., McMillan, D. E., Morin, F. L., & Demczuk, L. (2016). Effectiveness and experience of arts-based pedagogy among undergraduate nursing students: A mixed methods systematic review. *JBI Database of Systematic Reviews and Implementation Reports, 14*(11), 139-239 https://journals.lww.com/jbisrir/Abstract/2016/11000/Effectiveness_and_experience_of_arts_based.15.aspx

Scott, S. (2019). 67 quotes about overcoming adversity and challenges in your life. *Happier Human.* https://www.happierhuman.com/quotes-about-overcoming-adversity/

Seifter, H. (2016). Arts-based learning leads to improvements in creative thinking skills, collaborative behaviors and innovation outcomes. *The Art of Science Learning.* http://www.artofsciencelearning.org/phase2-research-findings/

Serbati, A., Aquario, D., Da Re, L., Paccagnella, O., & Felisatti, E. (2020). Exploring good teaching practices and needs for improvement: Implications for staff development. *Journal of Educational, Cultural and Psychological Studies (ECPS Journal), 0*(21), 43-64. https://doi.org/10.7358/ecps-2020-021-serb

Van Katwyk, T., Al-Azraki, A., & Kolahdouz Asfahani, S. (2019). Assessing the learning that occurs with arts-based pedagogy: Learning about social justice. *University of Waterloo.* https://uwaterloo.ca/centre-for-teaching-excellence/descriptions-funded-lite-grant-projects/assessing-learning-occurs-arts-based-pedagogy-learning-about

World Health Organization (2020, February12). *World experts and funders set priorities for COVID-19 research.* https://www.who.int/news/item/12-02-2020-world-experts-and-funders-set-priorities-for-covid-19-research

Chapter Seven:

How the Pedagogy of Kindness Can Accentuate the Advantages and Minimize the Limitations of Online Education

By Elizabeth Gorny-Wegrzyn

Chapter Seven investigates peer-reviewed and grey literature on how the PofK can accentuate the advantages and help minimize the limitations of online learning. The purpose of this chapter is to examine how educators can provide quality education in an online milieu and discuss possible solutions to online teaching and learning drawbacks. The literature revealed several strategies educators moving from face-to-face to online instruction could employ to help students overcome the limitations of the online milieu while maintaining quality education. Using pedagogies that utilize kindness, care, empathy, and compassion, like the PofK, helps overcome some of these limitations and helps to preserve high quality in online education. Additionally, this chapter describes how a PofK can accentuate the advantages of online education for teachers and learners.

Chapter Objectives

After completing chapter seven the reader will be able to

- Identify the advantages and limitations of online education
- Explain how PofK helps educators maintain quality education in an online milieu
- Outline strategies that educators and academic administrators use to mitigate the limitations of online learning
- Describe the pedagogies and teaching philosophies that can facilitate quality online education

Introduction/Background

"Online learning is not the next big thing, it is the now big thing." - Donna J. Abernathy (Pappas, 2014)

Distance learning, through correspondence colleges, first emerged in the mid-19th century with the advent of the US Postal Service (Visual Academy, 2021). Students communicated with teachers through the mail, sending the course materials back and forth between educators and learners (Visual Academy, 2021). With the development of the internet and digital technology, distance learning became increasingly high-tech and is presently a popular and sophisticated teaching approach in higher education that offers legitimate online courses and degrees (Visual Academy, 2021). Alshamrani (2019) defines online education as "a utilisation of multi-media technologies and the internet to improve the quality of learning. This can be implemented by creating an ease of access to the services and facilities on offer in addition to facilitating exchanges and collaborations from a distance. Online learning also refers to the use of advanced technologies which facilitate the access to online resources" (p. 15). In other words, online education utilizes technology to provide information to students and to facilitate communication in the teaching and learning process (Alshamrani, 2019).

At present, online education, or e-learning (using electronic communication to facilitate learning), is in demand due to its accessibility for all students, even those not living near an education facility. As well, online instruction is advantageous for those who prefer self-paced study. The flexibility to learn anywhere or at any time, day or night, allows students to continue accomplishing their work and family obligations while studying at their convenience (Alshamrani, 2019). Online education also opens up the global e-learning market, providing students with the opportunity to enroll at a college or university of their choice by removing the barrier of geographic location (Alshamrani, 2019). As well, e-learning brings together students from different countries, nationalities, and cultures and facilitates an open exchange of diverse viewpoints, life experiences, ideas, and beliefs (Bates. 2020; Squire, 2018). Further, the online approach allows educational institutions to recruit faculty from anywhere, ensuring that they hire the most deserving educators for each educational offering.

Online learning is relevant in our technological world. As discussed in Chapter Six, this is even more so now during the COVID-19 pandemic. The preventative measures put into place to help stop the spread of this deadly virus, specifically social distancing, necessitated the predominant teaching delivery in higher education to transition almost overnight from a face-to-face and blended teaching method to a completely online approach (Altbach & De Wit, 2020; Bates, 2020; Rapanta et al., 2020).

One and a half billion students worldwide took part in some distance learning during the height of the pandemic, and university administrators and faculty endeavoured to meet their educational needs (Contact North, 2020). Faculty in universities continued to provide quality education by increasing the accessibility of e-learning and creating online courses that engaged and motivated students (Contact North, 2020). Educators most familiar with teaching face-to-face had to quickly prepare themselves by learning new skills and adapting their instructional strategies to teach effectively in an online milieu. As noted in Chapter Six, this trend toward more education being offered online will likely continue post-pandemic.

Online education offers many advantages for learners, but some educators and learners still do not believe online learning is as effective as face-to-face instruction (Friedman, 2020; Mukhtar et al., 2020; University of Illinois, 2021). Further, some teachers and students feel e-learning presents barriers to effective studying and limitations to the delivery of top-quality education (Friedman, 2020; Mukhtar et al., 2020; University of Illinois, 2021). In this chapter, we address some of these concerns and point out how a PofK can help overcome some of these potential shortcomings.

The purpose of Chapter Seven is to examine current literature on how the PofK can accentuate the advantages and help minimize the limitations of online learning. We investigated how teachers can continue to deliver quality education in an online environment and then discuss and propose possible solutions to some of the identified e-learning limitations. This review is relevant since COVID-19 has forced a global lockdown in traditional in-class higher education and has compelled educators to transition from a face-to-face teaching method to an online approach. It is likely that even post-pandemic if some teaching institutions transition back to the face-to-face milieu, other academic establishments will continue to offer e-learning or a hybrid model. Contact North (2020) writes that the total and abrupt immersion into online learning due to the pandemic (and the new technologies and pedagogies associated with e-learning) already has academic institutions "exploring the implications of these developments for program and course delivery beyond the pandemic" (para. 6). Providing an appraisal of the advantages and limitations of online education and recommending

PofK help solve some of the e-learning shortcomings may benefit students and educators in overcoming perceived or actual limitations of online learning in the future. The literature consistently shows that educators deliver high-quality education when employing pedagogies that are collaborative and inviting to students. Teachers that use kindness, care, empathy, and compassion in their teaching philosophy enrich learning environments and meet educational goals.

Advantages of Online Education

Accessibility and Flexibility

Online instruction has revolutionized higher education. It has provided learners from around the globe with the opportunity to study in educational institutions of their choice and allowed them to continue working and attending to personal responsibilities while studying. Online learning enables students to access the global market in education which conventional face-to-face instruction limits (Appanna, 2008). Statistica (2021) estimates the global e-learning market will exponentially grow to over 370 billion U.S. dollars in the next five years, saying, "In 2019, the global online e-learning market was sized at approximately 101 billion U.S. dollars. During that same period, learning management system market generated roughly 18 billion U.S. dollars. By 2026, the total market for e-learning worldwide is forecasted to grow exponentially, reaching over 370 billion U.S. dollars" (p.1).

Through the present global e-learning model, students can live anywhere in the world and access course materials and class activities at any time (day or night) at their convenience (Distance-learning-college-guide.com., 2015; Gautam, 2020; University of Illinois, 2021). During the COVID pandemic, many working students lost access to childcare as schools and daycares were closed (National University, 2021). These same students often provided additional care to older parents and loved ones who could not leave their homes for groceries and medications. These extra family responsibilities further eroded the time adult working learners had to devote to their courses (National University, 2021). E-learning requires no commuting time or time out of the home, making it a more efficient way of learning during COVID-restricted experiences. Students who must provide childcare at home during the pandemic can continue their studies through an online mode (National University, 2021). The benefits of accessing

116

course material from home, the flexibility of studying at your own pace, and the convenience of no commute are three substantial advantages of online learning.

Student-Centred Teaching

Online education has soared in popularity because it provides an opportunity to continue student-centred learning for virtually any student in the world in the comfort of their own home. Online educators adapt their teaching strategies according to the unique needs and abilities of online students. These students come from diverse backgrounds and may have different cognitive levels, which require student-focused teaching approaches (Alshamrani, 2019; Bates, 2020). Student-oriented e-learning encourages active learning and adjusts according to each student's differences and individual learning goals (Bates, 2020; Rapanta et al., 2020; University of Illinois, 2021).

Many academics still consider face-to-face instruction superior to e-learning in delivering quality education, but they also criticize traditional classroom teaching for supporting passive learning (Rapanta et al., 2020). Conventional face-to-face instruction uses behaviourism as its primary teaching philosophy (Rapanta et al., 2020). Behaviourism is a learning theory based on scientific positivism. Behaviourists believe students learn when educators impart objective facts to them, usually through a lecture format (Alshamrani, 2019; Bates, 2019).

Online instruction, on the other hand, generally utilizes a philosophical perspective to teaching known as constructivism. Constructivism is a learning theory based on cognitive psychology that emphasizes that gaining knowledge through engaging learning interactions and mutual sharing of personal experiences and ideas is vital to the learning process (Alshamrani, 2019; Bates, 2019). Constructivism proposes that learning is an active process whereby individuals "generate knowledge and meaning from their experiences, mental structures, and beliefs that are used to interpret objects and events. Constructivism focuses on the importance of the individual knowledge, beliefs, and skills through the experience of learning" (Gogus, 2012, para. definition). In other words, constructivists surmise that students actively learn when they interpret information in the context of their own experiences and understand this new information by combining it with their prior knowledge (Alshamrani, 2019; Bates, 2019).

In the same sense, social constructivism is also commonly the foundation of online education. Social constructivism is the generation of ideas, collectively, by a group (Vygotsky, 1978). Educators who are proponents of this teaching philosophy use engaging instructional strategies that encourage interaction as part of the learning process (Alshamrani, 2019). Students can engage in class discussions with one another and with the teacher, and respond to dialogues most relevant to their interests, personal experiences, and learning needs (University of Illinois, 2021). In other words, social constructivist approaches are student-centred and invite learners to direct their own learning experience, make distinctive and valuable contributions to the class, and acquire knowledge relevant to them and their unique educational goals (University of Illinois, 2021). Therefore, it is critical for educators who move from face-to-face to online instruction to employ student-centred approaches to teaching. Teachers must be mindful of different learner abilities and individual learning goals and needs. Using pedagogies like a PofK can help engage students and facilitate their collaboration with class activities (Bates, 2020; Rapanta et al., 2020). By modifying instruction to be more student-centred, educators must rethink (and potentially adjust) their educational philosophies, teaching methods, and course designs. Teachers who adopt a PofK or other pedagogies that use kindness, care, empathy, and compassion as a teaching philosophy, facilitate student-centred teaching. A PofK recognizes students as active classroom partners and moves the focus from educators to learners and the co-creation of knowledge (Gilmour, 2021).

Anonymity as an Advantage to Online Education

Another crucial advantage of online education is anonymity. Often in e-learning, there are no visual indications of students' physical appearance, thus all students are potentially treated equally by the instructor and classmates. Everyone can contribute to class discussions and activities without fear of discrimination due to age, gender, race, disability, dress, etc. (Appanna, 2008; University of Illinois, 2021). Students are evaluated only on the content of their contributions and their understanding of course materials and may be motivated to participate more frequently without fear of prejudice (University of Illinois, 2021). Some introverted learners who may be quiet in a traditional learning environment and hesitant to express their ideas or to ask questions may find the veil of anonymity helps them find their voices in an online milieu (Appanna, 2008). Anonymity allows all learners to contribute more confidently and be judged solely on their ideas and expressions of knowledge.

Educators who embrace a PofK appreciate each learner's strengths and believe in potential. These teachers value diversity and strive for equity in facilitating learning with each person in the class. The advantage of the anonymity provided by the online milieu may aid teachers in enacting these values of a PofK.

Economic and Environmental Benefits

Online education also provides economic benefits to learners, teachers, and educational institutions. E-learning is more affordable for students, eliminating transportation costs, commuting, and buying course materials and books as many resources are open access learning resources without cost (Gautam, 2020). E-learning is also beneficial to academic institutions as universities and colleges eventually receive substantial returns from online courses despite the initial high startup costs (Appanna, 2008).

There are also potential benefits to the environment that can have positive economic outcomes. When students and teachers do not have to commute to colleges and universities, not only are transportation costs eliminated, but greenhouse emissions from cars and buses are also reduced (Gautam, 2020). Course materials for online education are electronic, and therefore the printing and shipping of textbooks is unnecessary (Distance-learning-college-guide.com., 2015; Gautam, 2020). Further, learners study at home, so physical infrastructure like academic buildings do not need to be constructed or heated/cooled (Gautam, 2020). The carbon footprint of education, and associated costs, are substantially reduced with e-learning making it a greener option.

A PofK focuses on equity in learning opportunities. The economic and environmental benefits of online education can help to mitigate the reality of educational inequality that manifests in such realities as school pushout and opportunity gaps. Educators who enact the values of a PofK fight against complacency that helps produce disparities and perpetuate the achievement gap (real or perceived) between different learners. Living a PofK requires educators to engage in uncomfortable conversations and call out inequities determined by economic disparities (Noguera, 2018). The economic advantages of online teaching and learning are helpful for educators striving to call out and reduce injustices.

Accessibility of Resources

Online education makes collaboration possible between students from diverse backgrounds and experiences (University of Illinois, 2021). Further, online instructors can access and invite international experts to join class discussions virtually without the barrier of physical location (Appanna, 2008; University of Illinois, 2021). For example, a distinguished author of a unique concept can become a "guest" speaker in an online class. Also, educators and students can access other academic institutions and libraries, scholarly articles, and course materials from anywhere and can revise or update data instantly (University of Illinois, 2021). Additionally, many e-learning resources are open access online publications. Open access resources are free for institutions, teachers, students, researchers, and the public, making them easily assessable at no cost to learners (UC Santa Barbara Library, 2019). Having quality learning resources instantaneously accessible at your fingertips at no cost is a benefit unique to electronic education. Open access resources that are current and appropriate for a course are a significant advantage for educators who believe in a PofK and desire equity in learning opportunities.

Student Satisfaction and Learning Outcomes

Finally, the online education process increases student satisfaction due to flexibility, accessibility, and affordability (Gautam, 2020). Student satisfaction is also positively affected by reliable technology, learner-centred instruction, and educators who facilitate and partner in the learning process (Bates, 2020; Hughes, 2020; Rapanta et al., 2020). Student-centred instruction encourages learners, peers, and educators to share the learning process as partners. This teaching strategy promotes interaction and open exchange of thoughts, values, and ideas that can motivate and engage students, produce higher student satisfaction, heighten social consciousness, and facilitate better learning outcomes (Bates, 2020; Houlden & Veletsianos, 2020; Hughes, 2020; Rapanta et al., 2020; Serbati et al., 2020). These values of collaboration, student-centeredness, interaction, and heighted social consciousness clearly align with the PofK.

Teachers can deliver quality education in an online environment if they prepare themselves appropriately, acquire new skills necessary for online instruction, and develop effective and interactive online teaching strategies. Empirical studies indicate many advantages to e-learning, including increased student satisfaction with the learning process, enhanced student engagement and motivation, heightened social awareness, and improved learning outcome achievements. Therefore, if educators use appropriate online teaching methods and apply teaching philosophies that use kindness, care, empathy, and compassion, e-learning can be as effective (or more effective) as face-to-face teaching and may provide many advantages.

Limitations to Online Education and Potential Solutions

Though there are many advantages to online education, we need to analyze and address its limitations. Through an analysis of e-learning limitations, we can hopefully develop workable solutions to some of the drawbacks, such as technological issues, students' lack of motivation, engagement and participation, and feelings of psychological isolation. It is proposed that a PofK helps to overcome some of the potential limitation of online education.

Technological Limitations of Online Education

Some of the most frustrating and inconvenient problems that arise in e-learning are technological issues. Online education is dependent on technology such as access to reliable internet, social media, computers, laptops, cellphones, etc. Students will not access their course materials to study and learn if there is a breach in internet connectivity, slow or unreliable internet, or any other technical problems (Alshamrani, 2019).

Technological issues can encompass a wide range of problems such as accessibility to technology, availability and affordability of reliable and high-speed internet and technical tools, internet connection disruptions, technical glitches in home computers or institution infrastructure, and lack of technological and computer literacy of academic staff and students (Alshamrani, 2019;

Friedman, 2020; Gautam, 2020; University of Illinois, 2021). Though these limitations to e-learning can significantly hamper the process of online education, there are several viable solutions to help mitigate these problems.

Potential Solutions to Technological Limitations

Several stakeholders must be involved when tackling the technological issues related to e-learning. Principal stakeholders include government representatives, policymakers, academic administrators, educators, learners, course designers, and technical experts (Alshamrani, 2019). While the solutions to technological issues require the involvement of multiple stakeholders, educators and students who engage in a PofK can also help mitigate this limitation.

Responsibilities of Governments and Policymakers

Government officials and policymakers must undertake the limitations of accessibility, availability, and affordability of fast and reliable internet technology to provide the foundation of e-learning. Education policies and frameworks that support the equitable expansion of telecommunication services, including for socioeconomically disadvantaged neighbourhoods and remote areas, must be enacted (Mukhtar et al., 2020; University of Illinois, 2021). Students and teachers need to access top-quality, affordable internet technology and expert technical support.

Responsibilities of Academic Administrators

Academic administrators need to make significant initial investments to upgrade the technological infrastructures of their institutions. These upgrades will facilitate smooth and reliable course delivery and ease navigation for students and instructors (Alshamrani, 2019; Appanna, 2008; Mukhtar et al., 2020). The base technological needs for course transmission include fast and reliable internet service, appropriate computer facilities for teachers and students, and suitable learning management systems (Alshamrani, 2019). As well, the technical support staff is essential to keep everything running smoothly. Alshamrani (2019) writes, "This increase in the technological base required also warrants the need for provisioning adequate support staff, who shall be responsible for the routine maintenance and upgrade of the technical infrastructure and to cater to the technological needs and support needs of the students and the instructors" (p. 35).

Responsibilities of Educators

Academic faculty need to acquire specialized skills and knowledge to deliver quality education in an online learning environment. Professors who usually teach face-to-face must be educated in online course instruction and design and be knowledgeable regarding software applications to help students navigate these systems (Alshamrani, 2019; Appanna, 2008; Gautam, 2020; Mukhtar et al., 2020). Further, educators must adapt their teaching strategies and create classes that are suitable for an online environment but can still motivate and engage students and facilitate class participation (Alshamrani, 2019; Appanna, 2008; Bates, 2019, 2020; Gautam, 2020; Houlden & Veletsianos, 2020; Mukhtar et al., 2020). Teaching strategies and learning design options that can help make e-learning classes engaging include using high-tech graphics and audio and video dialogue added to text discussions (Alshamrani, 2019; Kebritchi et al., 2017; Mukhtar et al., 2020). Also, employing pedagogies like a PofK or arts-based pedagogy (ABP) stimulates student curiosity, motivation, and participation in e-learning courses (Perry & Edwards, 2019; Rapanta et al., 2020; Serbati et al., 2020). These instructional strategies can help online educators provide quality education and engage students to improve learning outcomes.

Responsibilities of Students

Students must have basic computer literacy and be comfortable with technology to succeed in an e-learning environment (Alshamrani, 2019; Mukhtar et al., 2020). Learners must also take responsibility for alleviating problems by keeping open communication with teachers and technical support staff. Friedman (2020) suggests that students inform their instructors of computer malfunctions or connectivity interruptions as most teachers will be understanding and have a standby solution such as pre-recorded classes. Also, students should avail themselves of technical help through video tutorials or the institution's technical support team if they are having problems understanding or adapting to new digital tools (Friedman, 2020). Learners can openly discuss technological limitations and find potential solutions when teachers create a classroom environment where students feel valued and thus are comfortable sharing issues and concerns with the instructor. A PofK is a foundation for open communication in the class that is important for creative problem-solving to overcome limitations, including technological issues.

Responsibilities of Course Designers and Technical Experts

Course designers, whether instructors themselves or out-sourced experts, must consider the learning needs and goals and the technical abilities of the students when planning and creating course designs (Alshamrani, 2019; Bates, 2019, 2020; Gautam, 2020; Houlden & Veletsianos, 2020; Mukhtar et al., 2020). Importantly, courses must be student-centred (incorporating a constructivist teaching philosophy) to motivate and engage students and facilitate their continued participation (Houlden & Veletsianos, 2020; Mukhtar et al., 2020). Further, the technical support experts must make technology readily understood and easy to navigate and be available to assist learners and academic staff when problems arise (Houlden & Veletsianos, 2020; Mukhtar et al., 2020). The goal is to create online courses that are interesting, interactive, and delivered as efficiently and seamlessly as possible using technology appropriate for the teaching strategies and suited to the learners' skill levels. Such course design aligns with the approaches used by instructors who engage in a PofK.

Lack of Student Motivation, Engagement, and Participation in Online Classes

Another significant limitation to e-learning occurs when there is a lack of student motivation, engagement, and class participation. Several causes can produce these lacks: overly long classes that do not use interactive and engaging learning strategies, students' inability to focus on computer screens for long periods, distractions (social media and other websites), and time management difficulties (Friedman, 2020; Gautam, 2020; Mukhtar et al., 2020; University of Illinois, 2021). The responsibility to mitigate these limitations lies with both the educators and the learners. Again, educators who engage a PofK are aware of these potential limitations and create a classroom environment that helps to minimize or eliminate them.

Potential Solutions to Lack of Motivation, Engagement, and Participation

What Educators Should Do

To alleviate the lack of student motivation and engagement, educators must recognize that each student has different abilities, needs, and learning goals and create a learner-centred syllabus (Bates, 2020; Kebritchi et al., 2017). Educators whose primary teaching experience is face-to-face instruction must be open to gaining new skills and knowledge to become effective online educators. A student-centred environment enables collaboration among learners and between students and teachers and provides meaningful learning activities that engage and motivate students and stimulate class participation (Perry & Edwards, 2019; Serbati et al., 2020).

Teachers who espouse a philosophy based on a PofK (along with care, empathy, and compassion) can better meet the learning goals of students from diverse cultures and different learning abilities (Serbati et al., 2020; Thomas, 2019). The PofK empowers students to become active and equal participants in the learning process, engaging them in school activities and on issues of social injustice (Serbati et al., 2020; Thomas, 2019). Exemplary educators who use kindness in pedagogy create learning environments that are collaborative and inviting, stimulating student engagement, and enhancing learning outcomes (Serbati et al., 2020; Thomas, 2019). These outstanding teachers often use engaging teaching strategies like arts-based instruction.

Using a teaching strategy like arts-based instruction can help motivate and engage students, sustain continued participation in academic activities, heighten social consciousness, and improve learning outcomes (Perry & Edwards, 2019; Serbati et al., 2020; Van Katwyk et al., 2019). Boston University. (n. d.) defines arts-based learning as "the purposeful use of artistic skills, processes, and experiences as educational tools to foster learning in non-artistic disciplines and domains" (para. 1). Arts-based instruction stimulates learners' curiosity in online class activities, enhances learners' creativity and problem-solving skills, and helps students achieve solutions in imaginative and original ways (Carleton University, 2020; Perry & Edwards, 2019). A PofK makes students feel more worthy as learners and as human beings.

Therefore, to be successful and effective as online instructors, educators should use kindness, care, empathy, and compassion in pedagogy. Instructors must also implement teaching strategies that feature meaningful learning activities, are enjoyable and inviting, stimulate curiosity, and increase motivation and participation in the learning process.

What Students Should Do

Students who enroll in online courses need to be self-directed learners and possess a certain amount of self-discipline to maintain their motivation and regular participation (Mukhtar et al., 2020). The University of Illinois (2021) website notes that online, "students must be well organized, self-motivated, and possess a high degree of time management skills in order to keep up with the pace of the course" (Para. The students). Friedman (2020) urges students to establish a regular daily schedule (even if late at night is the most convenient time for them) and to find a quiet and productive working space in their home to complete their assignments. Also, students who focus on their learning goals and communicate regularly with teachers, classmates, and academic advisors (if needed) are more likely to maintain their motivation and engagement and increase their satisfaction with online class activities (Friedman, 2020).

Student's Sense of Isolation in Online Education

Another significant limitation to e-learning is the student's sense of isolation. Online learners are at a physical distance from academic institutions and therefore unable to physically interact with teachers and peers, and this lack of interaction may lead to feelings of social isolation (Gautam, 2020; Friedman, 2020). Social isolation can inhibit student motivation and satisfaction with online education and impedes effective learning causing poor learning outcomes and increasing student drop-out rates (Croft et al., 2010). Withdrawals from online programs negatively impact learners, peers, and teachers, and when students do not complete courses, it is also an economic hit for academic institutions (Croft et al., 2010).

Effective online teaching is not the same as effective face-to-face instruction. Not being physically present with learners requires teachers to develop and purposefully use instructional approaches that remove any sense of isolation an online learner may experience. Therefore, it is imperative to find viable solutions to help online students feel they are part of a community and not alone to ensure they continue their studies successfully.

Potential Solutions to Social Isolation

Martin and Bolliger (2018) write that "student engagement increases student satisfaction, enhances student motivation to learn, reduces the sense of isolation, and improves student performance in online courses" (Para. Abstract). Educators, therefore, must use several innovative strategies to increase student engagement and satisfaction and decrease feelings of student isolation. Teaching approaches that make the students and the instructor feel "real" to each other can help build a sense of community in distance learning. As noted earlier, a PofK focuses on the humanity of all involved in the educational experience. When students sense the teacher cares about them as fellow humans and show interest in personalizing their learning, the sense of social isolation can be reduced. These are approaches used by educators who enact a PofK.

Technologies that Lessen Social Isolation

Several technologies can effectively facilitate communication between online students, peers, and teachers and mitigate students' feelings of isolation. Whiteboards, chat rooms, blogs, discussion forums, videoconferencing, social networking, and emails can help students connect to peers and educators and share information, thoughts, and feelings (Croft et al., 2010; Distance-learning-college-guide.com., 2015; Gautam, 2020; Friedman, 2020; Muhktar et al. 2020). Learning management systems and videoconferencing options that can facilitate communication and help students feel they are part of a community include Zoom, Skype, Face Time, Microsoft Teams, Google Meet, Edmodo, Moodle, WebEx, and Adobe Connect (Croft et al., 2010; Gautam, 2020; Friedman, 2020; Muhktar et al. 2020).

For instance, Croft et al. (2010) write that empirical studies have demonstrated that blogs can create a sense of community among students and reduce feelings of psychological isolation: while online discussion forums can increase student engagement, critical analysis, and self-reflection. Technology facilitates communication, but it is the human element (the human connections between students, peers, and educators) that ameliorates students' social isolation, provides support and care, and produces a sense of belonging (Croft et al., 2010).

Pedagogies and Teaching Strategies that Lessen Social Isolation

Different pedagogies and teaching strategies can also reduce the psychological effects of isolation and make students feel like a part of a community. Pedagogies that engage students and allow them to participate in the learning and teaching process as partners can help decrease learners' feelings of isolation (Kebritchi et al., 2017; Rapanta et al., 2020). The pedagogy of hope or the PofK, for example, embraces a teaching philosophy that encourages a free exchange of ideas, independent thought, and teacher-student collaboration. (hooks, 2003; Rapanta et al., 2020; Serbati et al., 2020). These pedagogies empower students and engage them in academic and social activities, positively impact learning environments, improve learning outcomes, enhance social consciousness, and lessen learners' feelings of isolation (hooks, 2003; Rapanta et al., 2020; Serbati et al., 2020).

The literature also demonstrates that educators who use innovative, creative, and participatory teaching strategies can capture students' interest, stimulate their curiosity, and engage them in academic activities (Kebritchi et al., 2017; Rapanta et al., 2020). Arts-based teaching strategies can motivate and engage students, increase participation in online class activities, make learners feel they are part of a community, and decrease psychological isolation (Perry & Edwards, 2019).

The study by Perry and Edwards (2019) found that arts-based techniques like poetweet, photo pairing, reflective mosaic, and six-word story inspire students to reflect on and find a deeper meaning to course material. These techniques also facilitate the achievement of affective domain learning outcomes and decrease feelings of isolation. (Perry & Edwards, 2019). Perry and Edwards (2019) describe the beneficial effects of arts-based instruction. The authors write, "interaction, social presence, and the sense of community were enhanced when arts-based approaches were used, in part because they encouraged creativity, helped to build rapport among participants, personalized interactions, cultivated trust, and promoted learner control" (Para. 1).

Finally, arts-based teaching strategies also encourage students to incorporate their own experiences when discussing thought-provoking subjects (Van Katwyk et al., 2019). Learning activities that further discussion on power and privilege, thus enabling understanding of social injustices and enhancing social awareness, empower learners and reduce social isolation. (Van Katwyk et al., 2019). In sum, instruction based on a PofK creates stimulating and engaging learning environments, promotes independent and creative thought, encourages problem-solving, facilitates communication skills and academic achievement, decreases social isolation, and enhances social consciousness (Perry & Edwards, 2019; Van Katwyk et al., 2019).

Though Chapter Seven did not enumerate all the advantages and limitations of online education, it provided an overview of some of the principal elements of e-learning. This chapter also demonstrated how a PofK helps accentuate the advantages and overcome the limitations of online learning. A search of the current literature revealed teaching strategies and pedagogies like the PofK that can facilitate the continued delivery of quality education and viable solutions to limitations of online education.

Conclusion

The purpose of Chapter Seven was to explore the literature on the advantages and limitations of e-learning and investigate how teachers can continue to deliver quality education in an online milieu using a PofK. The search brought forth many advantages to online education, such as global accessibility to higher education, the flexibility of self-paced study, student-oriented teaching, anonymity, economic and environmental benefits, accessibility to resources, increased student satisfaction and improved learning outcomes (Bates, 2020; Gautam, 2020; Houlden & Veletsianos, 2020; Hughes, 2020; Rapanta et al., 2020; Serbati et al., 2020; University of Illinois, 2021). In sum, online education provides engaging and stimulating learning environments, facilitates improved academic achievement, and increases social awareness if educators are prepared and use effective online teaching strategies and pedagogies. In this case, e-learning can be just as effective as face-to-face instruction.

The search also yielded several limitations to e-learning and possible actions to lessen these limitations. The solutions to the technological drawbacks of e-learning took a concerted effort from many to help mitigate the constraints (Friedman, 2020; Gautam, 2020; Gandhi, 2019; University of Illinois, 2021).

The chapter also revealed that effective online teaching strategies and pedagogies that use kindness, care, empathy, and compassion could positively influence student motivation and engagement, sustained participation in online classes, and students' feelings of isolation. Communication technologies helped facilitate online interaction between students, peers, and educators (Croft et al., 2010; Gautam, 2020; Friedman, 2020; Muhktar et al., 2020). Whereas pedagogies (like the pedagogy of hope or the PofK) and instructional strategies (like arts-based instruction) motivated and engaged students in online class activities and made learners feel a part of a community, and lessened their feelings of isolation (hooks, 2003; Perry & Edwards, 2019; Rapanta et al., 2020; Serbati et al., 2020).

In summary, the literature shows that e-learning is a legitimate and valuable global educational method. Though online learning has limitations, many of these have workable solutions. Currently, due to COVID-19, the delivery of education has transitioned to an online milieu, and many educational institutions are already thinking of continuing an online or hybrid teaching approach post-pandemic. In periods of uncertainty, disruption, and anxiety (like during the COVID-19 pandemic), a pedagogical practice shaped by kindness and compassion can help build trust and equitable student-teacher relationships that facilitate optimal learning (Gilmour, 2021).

This examination of the advantages and limitations of e-learning can benefit educators and students presently teaching and studying in an online environment. Future research into finding the most effective solutions for the drawbacks of e-learning is paramount so that teachers can continue to provide high-quality education and so that students can continue to study effectively online. Promoting educators' use of a PofK can be a critical first step.

References

Alshamrani, M. (2019). An investigation of the advantages and disadvantages of online education. *Auckland University of Technology.* http://orapp.aut.ac.nz/bitstream/handle/10292/12479/AlshamraniMS.pdf?sequence=5&isAllowed=y

Altbach, P. G., & De Wit, H. (2020). Postpandemic outlook for higher education is bleakest for the poorest. *International Higher Education, 102,* 3–5. https://www.internationalhighereducation.net/api-v1/article/!/action/getPdfOfArticle/articleID/2904/productID/29/filename/article-id-2904.pdf

Appanna, S. (2008). A Review of benefits and limitations of online Learning in the context of the student, the instructor and the tenured faculty. *International Journal on E-Learning, 7*(1). 5-22

Bates, A. W. (2019). *Teaching in a digital age.* 2nd Edition. Vancouver: Tony Bates Associates. https://teachonline.ca/teaching-in-a-digital-age/teaching-in-a-digital-age-second-edition

Bates, A. W. (2020). Advice to those about to teach online because of the corona-virus. *Online Learning and Distant Education Resources.* https://www.tonybates.ca/2020/03/09/advice-to-those-about-to-teach-online-because-of-the-corona-virus/.

Boston University. (n. d.). Arts-based learning. *Center for Teaching and Learning.* https://www.bu.edu/ctl/guides/arts-based-learning/

Clegg, S., & Rowland, S. (2010). Kindness in pedagogical practice and academic life. *British Journal of Sociology of Education, 31*(6), 719-735. http://www.jstor.org/stable/25758494

Contact North. (August 04, 2020). A new pedagogy is emerging and online learning is a key contributing factor. *Teachonline.ca* https://teachonline.ca/tools-trends/how-teach-online-student-success/new-pedagogy-emerging-and-online-learning-key-contributing-factor

Croft, N., Dalton, A., & Grant, M. (2010) Overcoming isolation in distance learning: Building a learning community through time and space, *Journal for Education in the Built Environment, 5*(1), 27-64.

https://www.tandfonline.com/action/showCitFormats?doi=10.11120%2Fj
ebe.2010.05010027

Distance-learning-college-guide.com. (2015). *Advantages and disadvantages of distance learning.* http://www.distance-learning-college-guide.com/advantage-and-disadvantage-of-distance-learning.html

Friedman, J. (2020, May 04). Tackle challenges of online classes due to COVID-19. *U.S. News.* https://www.usnews.com/education/best-colleges/articles/how-to-overcome-challenges-of-online-classes-due-to-coronavirus

Gautam, P. (2020, October 10). Advantages and disadvantages of online learning. *eLearning Industry.* https://elearningindustry.com/advantages-and-disadvantages-online-learning

Gogus A. (2012) Constructivist Learning. In: Seel N.M. (eds) *Encyclopedia of the Sciences of Learning.* Springer, Boston, MA. https://doi.org/10.1007/978-1-4419-1428-6_142

hooks, b. (2003). *Teaching community: A pedagogy of hope.* New York: Routledge

Houlden, S., & Veletsianos, G. (2020). Coronavirus pushes universities to switch to online classes – but are they ready? *The Conversation.* https://theconversation.com/coronaviruspushes-universities-to-switch-to-online-classes-but-arethey-ready-132728.

Hughes, C. (2020). COVID-19, higher education and the impact on society: what we know so far and what could happen. *World Economic Forum.* https://www.weforum.org/agenda/2020/11/covid-19-higher-education-and-the-impact-on-society-what-we-know-so-far-and-what-could-happen/

Kebritchi, M., Lipschuetz, A., & Santiague, L. (2017). Issues and challenges for teaching successful online courses in higher education: A literature review. *Journal of Educational Technology Systems, 46,* 4-29. 10.1177/0047239516661713. https://www.researchgate.net/publication/319013030_Issues_and_Challenges_for_Teaching_Successful_Online_Courses_in_Higher_Education_A_Literature_Review

Martin, F., & Bolliger, D. (2018). Engagement matters: Student perceptions on the importance of engagement strategies in the online learning

environment. *Online Learning, 22*(1).
https://files.eric.ed.gov/fulltext/EJ1179659.pdf

Mukhtar, K., Javed, K., Arooj, M., & Sethi, A. (2020). Advantages, limitations and recommendations for online learning during COVID-19 pandemic era. *Pakistan journal of medical sciences, 36*(COVID19-S4), S27–S31. https://doi.org/10.12669/pjms.36.COVID19-S4.2785

National University. (2021). *Student parents: Balancing school, work, & child care during COVID-19.* https://www.nu.edu/resources/student-parents-balancing-school-work-child-care-during-covid-19/

Pappas, C. (2014, April 25). *23 Inspirational eLearning quotes for eLearning professionals.* https://elearningindustry.com/inspirational-elearning-quotes-for-elearning-professionals

Perry, B & Edwards, M. (2019). Innovative arts-based learning approaches adapted for mobile learning. *Open Praxis, 11*(3). https://doi.org/10.5944/openpraxis.11.3.967

Rapanta, C., Botturi, L., Goodyear, P. et al. (2020). Online university teaching during and after the Covid-19 crisis: Refocusing teacher presence and learning activity. *Postdigit Sci Educ, 2*, 923–945 https://doi.org/10.1007/s42438-020-00155-y

Serbati, A., Aquario, D., Da Re, L., Paccagnella, O., & Felisatti, E. (2020). Exploring good teaching practices and needs for improvement: Implications for staff development. *Journal of Educational, Cultural and Psychological Studies (ECPS Journal), 0*(21), 43-64. https://doi.org/10.7358/ecps-2020-021-serb

Squire, K. (2018). Innovation in times of uncertainty. *On The Horizon, 26*(1), 23-58. https://www.emerald.com/insight/content/doi/10.1108/OTH-07-2017-0051/full/html

Statistica. (2021). *Size of the global e-learning market in 2019 and 2026, by segment.* https://www.statista.com/statistics/1130331/e-learning-market-size-segment-worldwide/

Thomas, W. (2019, August 23). Pedagogy of care. https://willt486.github.io/teaching/2019/08/23/pedagogy-of-care/

UC Santa Barbara Library. (2019). *Should I publish in an open access journal?* https://www.library.ucsb.edu/scholarly-communication/should-i-publish-open-access-journal

University of Illinois. (2021). *Strengths and weaknesses of online learning.* https://www.uis.edu/ion/resources/tutorials/online-education-overview/strengths-and-weaknesses/

Van Katwyk, T., Al-Azraki, A., & Kolahdouz Asfahani, S. (2019). Assessing the learning that occurs with arts-based pedagogy: Learning about social justice. *University of Waterloo.* https://uwaterloo.ca/centre-for-teaching-excellence/descriptions-funded-lite-grant-projects/assessing-learning-occurs-arts-based-pedagogy-learning-about

Visual Academy. (2021). The history of online schooling. *Onlineschools.org.* https://www.onlineschools.org/visual-academy/the-history-of-online-schooling/Article

Vygotsky, L. (1978). *Mind in Society.* London: Harvard University Press

Chapter Eight:

Lessons for Educators who Seek to Adopt and Enact a Pedagogy of Kindness

By Elizabeth Gorny-Wegrzyn

Chapter Eight provides a short conclusion to this book. The purpose of this chapter is to summarize key lessons learned and take-away messages from the book that practicing educators who strive to adopt and enact a PofK can use immediately. In these times of uncertainty and potential anxiety created by multiple challenges and changes in the world, it is essential that learning continues, and that education has value for students, educators, and society. There are many ways that a PofK can make teaching and learning optimally effective.

Chapter Objectives

After completing Chapter Eight the reader will be able to

- Utilize principles of PofK in their teaching practice
- Describe why a PofK to strengthens success in online and face-to-face teaching
- Discuss the links between PofK and positivity, mindfulness, and gratitude in pedagogy
- Suggest teaching strategies that are aligned with a PofK

This book is a compilation of literature searches, knowledge, and personal experiences related to kindness in pedagogy. The PofK is a successful teaching philosophy that helps students and educators flourish in their academic and personal lives. The theoretical underpinnings of the PofK come from a teaching philosophy that encourages students to be autonomous and to share authority with teachers while discouraging hierarchal power structures in academia (Magnet et al., 2014; McLeod, 2019; Western Governors University, 2020). The belief that students and teachers are equal partners in the educational process instills feelings of worth, self-reliance, and motivation in learners and helps them achieve academic and personal success (Perry & Edwards, 2012; Serbati et al., 2020).

Educators who embrace pedagogies that have strong links to the foundations of the PofK, such as the Invitational Learning Theory or OP, incorporate kindness, care, empathy, compassion, positivity, mindfulness, and gratitude into their practice and create learning environments that are open and inviting to students (Brunzell et al., 2016; Henard & Roseveare, 2012; Purkey & Novak, 2015). Understanding that students are individuals and honouring that they have distinctive characteristics and unique prior experiences and knowledge, accommodates their specific learning needs and facilitates academic success (Brunzell et al., 2016; Clegg & Rowland, 2010; Magnet et al., 2014).

Educators who use creative teaching strategies, like arts-based instruction, engage students more fully and make their learning more meaningful by allowing them to draw upon their prior experiences in this process. These teaching strategies facilitate students' affective domain learning outcomes achievement and encourage discussions on human feelings, values, attitudes, and biases (Perry & Edwards, 2019).

The literature consistently shows that educators who embrace a PofK and who use innovative teaching methods nourish the unique needs of students and make them achieve more academically. These exceptional teachers also nurture students' personal lives by making them feel worthy as humans while challenging them to look outside their viewpoints and to appreciate and value others. Finally, educators espousing a PofK also benefit by being more successful and satisfied in their work.

We believe all educators should partner with students and share equally in the teaching/learning process. Building student/teacher relationships based on equality, respect, and trust and having learner-centred education can benefit everyone. Instilling strength of character, tolerance, social consciousness, and confidence in students makes them better citizens and kinder human beings. Though one of the goals of education is to prepare individuals to become productive members of society, would not it be wonderful if these successful citizens were also kind, empathetic, caring, and compassionate?

References

Brunzell, T., Stokes, H., & Waters, L. (2016). Trauma-informed positive education: Using positive psychology to strengthen vulnerable students. *Contemporary School Psychology, 20*, 63-83. https://doi.org/10.1007/s40688-015-0070-x

Clegg, S., & Rowland, S. (2010). Kindness in pedagogical practice and academic life. *British Journal of Sociology of Education, 31*(6), 719-735. https://doi.org/10.1080/01425692.2010.515102

Gray, A. (n. d). Constructivist teaching and learning. *University of Saskatchewan.* https://saskschoolboards.ca/wp-content/uploads/97-07.htm#EXECUTIVE%20SUMMARY

Henard, F., & Roseveare, D. (2012). *Fostering quality teaching in higher education: Policies and practices.* Paris: OECD.

Magnet, S., Mason, C., & Trevenen, K. (2014). Feminism, pedagogy, and the politics of kindness. *Feminist Teacher, 25*, 1-22. https://doi.org/10.5406/femteacher.25.1.0001

McLeod, S. (2019). Constructivism as a theory for teaching and learning. *Simply Psychology.* https://www.simplypsychology.org/constructivism.html

Perry, B., & Edwards, M. (2012). Creating an "invitational classroom" in the online educational milieu. *American Journal of Health Sciences (AJHS), 3*(1), 7-16. https://doi.org/10.19030/ajhs.v3i1.6747

Perry, B & Edwards, M. (2019). Innovative arts-based learning approaches adapted for mobile learning. *Open Praxis, 11*(3). https://doi.org/10.5944/openpraxis.11.3.967

Purkey, W. W., & Novak, J. M. (2015). An introduction to invitational theory. *invitationaleducation.org* https://www.invitationaleducation.org/wp-content/uploads/2019/04/art_intro_to_invitational_theory-1.pdf

Serbati, A., Aquario, D., Da Re, L., Paccagnella, O., & Felisatti, E. (2020). Exploring good teaching practices and needs for improvement: Implications for staff development. *Journal of Educational, Cultural and Psychological Studies (ECPS Journal), 21*, 43-64. https://doi.org/10.7358/ecps-2020-021-serb

Western Governors University. (2020, May 27). *What is constructivism?* https://www.wgu.edu/blog/what-constructivism2005.html#close

Acknowledgements by Elizabeth Gorny-Wegrzyn

I want to give a heartfelt thank you to all the people who helped bring this book, *Pedagogy of Kindness: Changing Lives, Changing the World*, to fruition.

I want to thank my dear family, whose love and support are always with me through every endeavour.

I want to thank Anna Rothman, Editor & Publications Coordinator from Generis Publishing, who offered me this unique and exciting opportunity that I could never have imagined would come my way!

I also want to thank the outstanding educators who graciously agreed to help me with this project. Thank you, Regan Hack, Katherine Janzen, Dr. Collen Stanton, and Dr. Beth Perry, for each uniquely contributing to a work based on the foundations of the Pedagogy of Kindness. Educators like you, who espouse a pedagogy of kindness in their teaching philosophy and live it in their lives, understand that being kind when sharing a learning experience with students can forever change their lives for the better. I thank you all sincerely for your valuable contributions to this book.

I especially want to thank Dr. Beth Perry, an exceptional educator epitomizing excellence in teaching and embracing kindness, care, compassion, and empathy as her philosophies in all aspects of her life. I cannot thank you enough for all you have done for me. From the moment I met you as my professor in Athabasca, to when you offered me a job as your research assistant, to when I thought of you as my colleague and then as my friend, you have been inspirational in my life.

Dear Beth, you have enabled me to be involved in so many enriching experiences and be successful at them through your continued encouragement and positive reinforcement. All the accomplishments in the past year are due to your mentorship and support.

The realization of this book is due to your motivation. You encouraged me to try, and then you helped by co-writing chapters, brainstorming ideas, proofreading and editing, and bringing cohesion to the themes. Your input has been invaluable. Thank you, Beth. I'm so grateful.

Before her untimely death Colleen Stanton, one of the authors of this book, wrote the following acknowledgement that we include in her memory. Colleen wrote, "Some of the most recent mentors that really influenced my thinking about how we can create health promoting, continuous learning, sustainable systems include: Dr. Carol Rolheiser (collaboratives, communities, teaching and learning, use of technology, online learning); Dr. Trevor Hancock (healthy sustainable communities, cities and planet); Dr. Jack Miller (holistic learning); Dr. Ardra Cole (qualitive research, arts-based research and lived experience); Dr. Ken Leithwood (distributed/shared leadership); Dr. Bud Hall (critical consciousness and social change); Dr. Fritjof Capra (living systems, complexity and consciousness); Dr. Gareth Morgan (Images of Organization); Dr. Beth Perry (visionary in online learning, art-based education. pedagogy of kindness); Elizabeth Gorny-Wegrzyn (author, pedagogy of kindness); and Dr. Margaret Edwards (visionary in online programme development, pedagogy of kindness) to name a few."

Printed in Great Britain
by Amazon

25931729R00079